LEAVING THE WITNESS

LEAVING THE WITNESS

Exiting a Religion and Finding a Life

AMBER SCORAH

VIKING

VIKING

An imprint of Penguin Random House LLC
penguinrandomhouse.com

Excerpts from transcripts of "Dear Amber" podcasts used
by permission of ChinesePod LLC.

Excerpts from "Mind Control in Twenty Minutes" by Patrick Mark Dunlop.
Reprinted by permission of the author.

9780735222540 (hardcover)
9780735222564 (ebook)

Printed in the United States of America
1   3   5   7   9   10   8   6   4   2

Designed by Amanda Dewey

Penguin is committed to publishing works of quality and integrity. In that spirit,
we are proud to offer this book to our readers; however, the story,
the experiences, and the words are the author's alone.

For Karl

The great enemy of the truth is very often not the lie—deliberate, contrived, and dishonest—but the myth—persistent, persuasive, and unrealistic. . . . We enjoy the comfort of opinion without the discomfort of thought.

—JOHN F. KENNEDY, Commencement Address at
Yale University, delivered June 11, 1962

It's great to be here. It's great to be anywhere.

—KEITH RICHARDS

The first thing I saw when I arrived in Shanghai was a fight on the street. People had extracted themselves from the masses on all sides to watch, standing like awkward party guests. Cyclists held up their black bicycles by the handlebars, pedestrians dallied, their hands full of thin plastic bags from the market. As the momentum of the city pushed against those who were stationary, people spilled over onto the street, like water around rocks. Our taxi driver slowed the car to look.

In the center of the crowd, a man and a woman were arguing. The people who had paused to take in this (as I would come to learn) common spectacle were silent as the parties involved shouted, laying out their dispute. No fist was raised—though fights on the street were common in Shanghai, at least in those days when tension felt so high, they rarely came to blows—and no intervention was undertaken by the crowd. But the two piqued bodies were electric, their muscles tensed with adrenaline and the faces above them contorted in pent-up anger.

This restraint was more arresting than a punch or shove

would have been. A slap of flesh to cheekbone would have provided a moment of relief; a blow would have forced a climax, a gasp, some kind of release, after which the paused city could transform itself back into its loud moving swarm. Bodies would move on, shopping bags would sag to rest on kitchen counters. But this simmering, unrequited tension, it was in the bones of the place. It boiled in arguments on streets, in the alleys of the hutongs sitting stubbornly in the shadows of the developers who waited to bulldoze them, and in the posture of the old men who spat at the ground as a Ferrari passed. It was a pressure that surrounded you and lodged in your head and became your own tension. If ever a place set the stage for a confrontation of any kind, Shanghai did: a theater in which you were occasionally the spectator in the crowd, or, by turns, the person in the middle, fighting.

Things hadn't blown up for me yet, of course. My husband and I had just come in over the Lupu Bridge from the airport, and on the smooth white polyester backseat of a taxi we had been whisked through six lanes of light green taxis and loaded trailer trucks, over shining new bridges full of a thousand years of promise looking down at the slow-moving, ancient brown rivers. Our car was in the old concessions of Shanghai when we came across this scene, creeping among a patchwork of crumbling European architecture bordered by bland high-rise complexes, all skirted by the life and labor that kept twenty million people eating, moving, and surviving in a metropolis that seemed to have no end, and no discernible way out.

For me, there was no excitement like that which could be generated by a move around the world. This was the third time

I had done it. Swapping a life in one place for a new life in another created an energy capable of invigorating even people like us, who were tired of living with each other. I had begged my husband to move to China for years. I was not allowed to leave him, so perhaps if I left enough places with him, it would suffice.

And I had longed for China. I had dreamed of being here so audibly and adamantly that the dream drove me into Chinese class and came out of my mouth contorted in the form of sounds like "zh," "xi," and "yun"—articulations that made my cheek muscles ache with the effort. My husband wasn't one for dreaming on his own, and he was content where he was, but I yearned for China like a death drive.

In the eyes of all the people I cared about, I ended up just that: dead.

But my goal was not death, it was life—other people's lives. I had been trying to save lives seventy hours a month for years as a missionary of sorts (what we called "pioneering") in my hometown of Vancouver, Canada, knocking at doors to warn people, people who didn't care, doors that opened (if they opened at all) to disdain, to anger, to apathy, and in the best cases, to a sort of bemused tolerance. I had dedicated my life to save from a fiery Armageddon the inhabitants of my self-satisfied West Coast city, a population of people who cared very little about the impending death they faced.

This unwelcomed work was made easier because I had friends who did it with me, and we went door-to-door, in all weather, drinking Starbucks coffees and noting down who was not at home on our Watchtower-issue lined paper sheets, returning the next week to more closed doors, indulging in an occasional smugness, knowing that they would regret their apathy one day. It was work without pay but done alongside eight million people around the world who were trained week in and week out, and all believed exactly the same things I had been taught as a little girl.

As futile as this work might sound, we had given up any thought of building a life in the world we had been born into, because this world was ending. Soon we would live in paradise, on Earth, and God would bring destruction on those who were not of our faith. It was our duty to save them, or if not save, at least warn them. We were very invested in the trade-off we had made. We gave up any hope of a career, or education, financial security, and certain relationships, all for the sake of saving these people, and goddammit—no pun intended—we were very concerned about their impending destruction. You wanted to save just one of these uppity, self-satisfied people for your trouble. I can use the "we" and speak with such certitude of a collective of over eight million people because we all believed without a shadow of a doubt that this paradise would soon be ours.

And thus, week by week, I took the card given to me by the elders in the congregation, on which was a map of the territory I was to cover, and was assigned a partner to work with. I went door-to-door, preaching throughout my community, giving my sermons, handing out my publications, and noting down house numbers and symbols on the lined record forms tucked into the map's plastic pouch. "NH" for not home. "B-CA" for busy, call again. "DNC" for do not call (if someone was especially threatening). Those householders who told me that they weren't interested or, worse yet, hid behind the curtain, pretending they weren't home, I simply scratched off till the next month, when they'd get another chance.

In this way, I kept knocking, surprised every year that I was still here in this doomed world, and that these people in the big houses were still alive. In time, I discovered that Chinese immigrants in my city were slightly more willing to hear me out, and I began to try to learn their language so as to teach them "the truth." I derived meaning from the busy activity of my life and from my friends in the close community of fellow preachers around me. The organization and these people and this service were what held my life in place and gave it its purpose, even if no one listened. I had been trained from birth to never stray from this hub of belief, this safety. My life depended on it.

Given the possibility that I might meet one interested person in these thousands of hours of preaching, I did a lot of preparation. I attended the five required meetings a week held in our congregation, where we studied the Bible and were trained in how to convert people to our interpretation of it. I read all the appointed materials and underlined the correct answers to questions cited below the paragraphs. Who the author of these materials was, I did not know, other than that the writings came from a Governing Body of men in Brooklyn who were the unquestioned leaders of us, God's people, men whose duty it was to give us our spiritual food at the proper time.

Our meetings followed the same structure every week, and were the same around the world. The conductor of the meeting read out the questions from a magazine written by the Governing Body. No matter what the question—be it "Why does God permit suffering?"—the paragraph had the answer. Was the question "Why do we die?" We had all the answers to the unsettling aspects of being human there in our literature. The brother asking the questions was so good at reading the questions, he became convinced, no doubt, that he was questioning. And studying hard, we found the answers we wanted there before us. This constant study and easy answers to any and all questions was satisfying, a luxury available only to the indoctrinated, and I won't say I don't miss it, like any luxury to which one has become accustomed.

This kind of peace of mind bred a certain self-confidence, a certainty of purpose. I did not fear leaving my home and moving far away, to this Communist country, a place where my religion had been banned since the 1950s, a place where those who went against the government were frequently "disappeared" or executed. I was doing God's will, and even if I died for doing it, I would have life everlasting on a paradise Earth *after* all those self-satisfied worldly people were killed.

And so I was in China on this day in 2005, riding in a taxi, our suitcases in the trunk packed with Bibles stuffed into socks and study books shoved into pairs of underwear. We knew very little about how our religion functioned here, if it did at all. The brothers in charge in Hong Kong who had approved us to come and serve here had simply told us that everything would be made clear, but not until we arrived. I knew nothing about how we would worship and preach in Shanghai, or what my life would look like, because anyone who knew was forbidden to tell so as not to endanger the people doing the work. As we carved our way between the rows and rows of vehicles and I looked at the thousands of faces we passed, I wondered how many Jehovah's Witnesses, foreign and local, might be in this city.

The taxi turned into a driveway and we found ourselves in a drop-off area surrounded by eight massive buildings holding up the lives of thousands of people lived midair, buttressed on all sides by hundreds of other buildings that looked more or less like them.

Our friends Jay and Emma had come to China a couple months before us, also to preach. Before that, the four of us had lived in Taiwan for three years; we had moved there to improve our limited Mandarin. My husband and I had arrived in Taipei at the peak of the SARS epidemic, and rented a room from a sister in the congregation who had been left the apartment by her blind parents. She and her sister lived in the dark, even though they could see—the windows were blacked out, and the sisters rarely turned a light on.

There was a special kind of terror in the air during the SARS outbreak in Taiwan. I understood very little Chinese at that time but knew enough to recognize the character for "death" (with a number beside it that grew larger every day) on the large TV in our furnished bedroom, which we were glued to while watching the nightly news. One evening a clip of people waving white towels from the windows of a hospital was broadcast. They had been put into quarantine, due to SARS cases among patients and staff, and the people were desperate because they were not being allowed out. The next morning, on the bus to my Chinese class, I saw that same hospital out the window, just a few blocks from our place.

We spent our time in Taipei improving our Chinese, preaching, and doing Bible studies with people who were patient enough to listen to our terrible Chinese. We went to Chinese class two hours a day, supporting ourselves by tutoring English. Eventually my husband and I moved into a *dinglou* apartment (housing that had been built as an afterthought atop an apartment building, because there was nowhere left in Taipei to build but upward). The external walls were made of metal, covered on the inside by wood paneling. Inside these walls, mice would run back and forth in the evening, swinging from the various electrical cords like they were vines. This apartment was as bright as the last one was dark, with the intense summer sun bringing the indoor temperatures up to a hundred degrees or more. The metal wall in the kitchen that had been left unpaneled was so hot I threw a raw egg on it once, to see if it would cook. It did, sort of.

The Taiwanese are welcoming to foreigners and were very good to us. The Taiwanese brothers and sisters knew we were on training ground to one day preach on the Chinese Mainland. God had said that the good news would be preached in all the Earth before the end came, and China was one of the last frontiers. We knew that was why the brothers and sisters in Taiwan helped us so much with the language, which I do not doubt was a painful task for them. A Westerner learning Chinese is like someone singing every line of a twangy country song out of tune. The foreigner believes he is communicating something, but that is only because he lives in a nation of kind, welcoming people whose deference and hospitality keep them from letting on that what the foreigner is saying to them is basically indecipherable. An English speaker learning Chinese sounds much worse than a Chinese person learning English, of that I am sure.

But they did this because being Taiwanese, they knew that they could never safely enter China on a mission to preach. They wanted those in China to hear the truth of God's kingdom; it was God's will, so they invested their time and energy to help us get there. It wasn't that being a Christian was illegal in China—there are a handful of Christian churches that the government permits to operate, albeit under its close governmental watch and subject to its approval. But Jehovah's Witnesses had no such permit and was one of the many religious groups operating underground in China illegally. It was a brazen act to come and preach, but someone from the West ran far fewer risks than someone from elsewhere. A Taiwanese thrown into a prison in China would be a lot less likely to get out than an American or a Canadian or a European. Knowing we had a better chance of success than they did, brothers and sisters in Taiwan took it as their duty to correct our tones (very bluntly), since no one else would, and set us off on our way to the Mainland with simplified Chinese literature, when the time was right.

The taxi had now pulled down the lane to the part of the complex Jay and Emma lived in, and we got out and paid the driver (who had earlier argued with us when we said we were moving to China: "You were in China," he said of Taiwan). We pulled out our luggage from the trunk—we each had only twenty pounds of worldly possessions, as that was all the airline allowed coming from Hong Kong, our stopover point, because there were no direct flights between Taiwan and the Mainland. We picked up the bags and found our way through a tiny courtyard, past a giant bicycle parking lot, and up to the building. We pressed the elevator button. Slowly, the car took us to the sixth floor, and when the door opened, Jay and Emma, the only souls we knew in this new country, were both standing there in their doorway, the fluorescent light and air-conditioning pouring outward, giving us a cold welcome to the large apartment behind them.

"Here we are," Emma said and laughed in the warm, belly-laugh way she had. It felt a little unreal to be here together, finally. We had all started Chinese class in Vancouver just four years ago, when China had seemed like a mystery, and now, yes, here we were.

The entire apartment was beautiful, much nicer than anywhere we had lived in Taipei. Emma and Jay had a way of making their home feel like a place where you'd like to relax and hang out, much more than my husband and I had ever been able to. There were shiny faux-hardwood floors, spacious, freshly painted walls, and all new fixtures. Leather sofas with gathered backs sat opposite a black lacquered kitchen table and chairs, all of which had come with the place. Gin, tonic water, ice, and limes sat on the table. It was a relief to know that these items were available in Shanghai (we were often thankful that Jesus had made water into wine in the Bible, because it solidified our right to drink, in moderation, of course). After having dinner and catching up, we went to bed in the spare room, hearing the clangs of late-night dishes being done in the apartments across the well between the buildings as we fell asleep.

The next morning, I rose early and went to the bathroom to shower. It was a large room, large enough that I was starting to get the feeling that this apartment was not designed for a childless couple but rather for a generation or two of a family to share. The bathroom tile was new, but the toilet was stained brown inside. It was the water that seemed to be rusty, and no amount of scrubbing could make it clean. It was like many things built in Shanghai in that era. They looked beautiful and shiny on the outside but were crumbling from the inside out because of poor construction and the pollution.

I turned on the tap, and the showerhead shrieked to life under the strong water pressure. I could hear sounds from the traffic outside over the spray. I took off my T-shirt and underwear and stood next to the patterned frosted glass of the window in the thick warmth of the un-air-conditioned room for a moment. Standing there naked, I couldn't see the street, and the window didn't open, but the flash of light green taxis flitting by filled in the flat spaces in the glass. In the white morning light of the city, their persistent honks were the welcome to a new home I hadn't yet seen in the light of day, and one that wouldn't give me any peace and quiet for a long time to come.

I took a shower and toweled off with the identical IKEA

towels we had all bought successively in each country we had lived in and left behind when we left, and went out to join the others for breakfast, my long hair dripping down my back, not drying in the humidity.

THERE WAS A PROTOCOL upon arriving in a country like this, where Jehovah's Witnesses were banned. Even if you knew someone doing the work there, as we did, you were told nothing about how the preaching was done, or how we would get together for meetings, until you were contacted by the brother who looked after "intake" and training.

Around the breakfast table, Jay outlined a game plan: since we couldn't tag along with them to preach, we would use our time this week to try and find a place to live, as our first order of business. Jay told us we also had to go to the local police station and register, as all foreigners were required to do every time they entered the country, or moved house. The brother who would instruct us on our next steps had our contact information from the branch office in Hong Kong, and would be in touch with us somehow, soon.

Emma took the morning off to walk with us around the neighborhood and help us get our bearings in order to figure out where we wanted to live. Their apartment was on the periphery of the French Concession, so we crossed the main road, Xujiahui Lu, and walked past a large construction site into the wobbly grid of houses built by the French in the mid-1800s, where there were a lot of shops and services. Nowadays most of the buildings had become skewed in spots, from repair made on top of repair, and they wore the years of weather in rounded edges, missing pieces of fascia, and colors faded to the hues of sun-bleached cars.

We walked along Sinan Road. Two-story town houses were lined up in rows with leaning exteriors and porous interiors that seemed to have made themselves part of the street outside. Out the windows, here and there, a long pole held the morning's wash, which had been hung to dry in the thick haze of the day. There was about a day's worth of clothes on each pole, hinting at the number of dwellers inside and their tastes. As we passed a mildewy stone house with orange Creamsicle-colored shutters, a woman carried a metal chamber pot out the front door and dumped it over the edge of the sidewalk.

At the corner, the ground felt greasy and my feet twisted under me as we passed in front of a restaurant: the sidewalk was covered in cooking oil from leftovers tossed straight onto the street. I noticed that all the main streets we passed had fenced-off bike lanes.

"Most of the friends get around by subway or buses here, because the city is so huge," Emma told us. "Cabs are pretty cheap, though. We've just been taking cabs or walking, mostly."

I already missed Taiwan, and with a pang of longing I thought of the freedom of my little purple bike, which I had left behind. But good to know there were fellow preacher "friends" here, that being the term used in China for what we called "brothers and sisters" everywhere else.

We turned left onto Fuxing Lu to the real estate office

Emma and Jay had used to find their place. My husband opened the door and the air-conditioning dried up our sweat in one gust.

Though Emma had come to Shanghai a few months earlier than us, my husband and I had been in Taiwan longer than she and Jay had been, and I was still the most fluent in Mandarin of the three of us, my Taiwanese teacher once singling me out in class and proclaiming, pointing at me: "You, Tai Tai (Mrs.). You will be fluent in Mandarin in two years," Then, pointing at another classmate, "You, no."

A man at a desk in the real estate office looked up at us with surprise, and after saying hello in Mandarin, I asked if there was someone we could talk to, to see their rental listings.

The man then addressed Emma, who hadn't spoken, but who was Japanese Canadian, and therefore perhaps looked more like someone who would understand him, asking her what kind of place we were looking for.

Emma didn't catch what he said, so I answered. The man sat back and digested it for a minute.

"Whoa, you speak Chinese," he said in English, pointing at me and looking at his colleague at the next desk, who was talking to a middle-aged Chinese couple. "Her Chinese is better than yours!" He laughed, switching over to Mandarin, pointing to the colleague. It wasn't true, but it was a common joke. The colleague and his customers stopped their conversation and looked over.

"Right, right, right, so incredible!" the colleague responded with a hearty laugh. The couple, easily distracted from their transaction, joined in and asked where we were from.

"Canada," I responded.

"Ah, Canada! You know Da Shan?" they asked me. Da Shan is a nerd from Saskatchewan who moved to China about twenty years ago, got married to a local, learned perfect Mandarin, and is now a celebrity.

"Nope, don't know him," I said. It was the first of the thousands of times I would have this conversation in China.

"But you are Taiwan-ren? You sound Taiwanese," the wife said. "*Niangniang quiang*—'little girl accent,' we call it."

For me, too, the change in accent between here and Taiwan was very pronounced. After three years in Taiwan, I was used to drawing out each syllable of a word, and adding accent words as punctuation at the end of each thought. Here, the Chinese was clipped, with parts of words nearly left unsaid, gravelly in quality and masculine. It was said that all the Western men who learned Chinese in Taiwan sounded effeminate to the Mainlanders. This might have been because every Chinese teacher in Taiwan was a woman, at least as far as I had seen, so these men were picking up a woman's way of speaking, but it also could have been because the Taiwanese Chinese, much like their society, was softer and gentler.

Work in the office was now at a standstill; the shock of a white woman speaking Chinese was one thing, but sounding like a Taiwanese person on top of it was fascinating. Someone held a phone receiver dangling away from their mouth while staring at us, still on a call.

"Okay, okay, okay, let me see what we have." The clerk pulled out a book that had sheets of paper held in plastic sleeves and flipped through, asking us what our budget was, did we want a new house or was an old house okay, what area, how many people, furnished or not. "Let me take down your number and I will call you." If he was surprised at how low our budget was compared to your average expat's, he didn't show it. We gave him Emma's number, as we had yet to get SIM cards for our cell phones; that was next on the list. We said our goodbyes and headed to the convenience store up the street.

After a week of exploring on foot, having the same conversations with real estate agents, chuckling along about Da Shan, and waiting for calls on new phone numbers so long we couldn't remember them ourselves, we found a place ten minutes away from Emma and Jay's by cab. It was in a pink-colored apartment complex I presumed was built in the 1950s, but like many buildings here, it had not aged well—I later found out it was actually built in the 1990s. This little afterthought of dwellings had been constructed at the end of a long alley we entered at the corner between a XinJiang noodle place and a carpenter's shack, a five-floor walkup with an iron fence that kept out the old houses that leaned in around it. At the time, it was an everyday sight, this kind of alley with this kind of life inhabiting it, but seeing it now in my memory, the beauty of it makes me tingle. I hope my neighbors are all still there, squatting on the curb to rest, frying up the hand-pulled noodles in the wok on the grease-covered sidewalk, the building superintendent in the booth at the gate writing down in a book every time someone went in or went out. I'd love to open up the book from 2005 and see what she had written about us.

We moved in the next day. The apartment was furnished, like most apartments we had seen, and quite a bit smaller than

Emma and Jay's, but it was clean and had been freshly reno-
vated. The rooms had all been painted a bright pink—it was
like living in the guts of a fish. There was a tan cotton love seat
in the tiny square living room, and two small bedrooms off the
living room at perpendicular openings. We set up the smaller
room as a computer room and a guest room, as there was a
futon in it. The larger bedroom in the back was ours, with
a giant wooden hutch covering one wall, for use as a closet, a
queen size bed, and a large TV. Off the back of the bedroom
was a line of windows, beyond which there was a small enclosed porch for hanging clothes to dry.

We spent the first few days smiling at our curious neighbors
as we climbed the stairs and they looked at us through the
metal grilles on their doors, taking cabs back and forth between IKEA and home, getting the basics we needed for a
household, and trying all the food in the neighborhood.

It was a very traditional Shanghainese block—you didn't
see too many foreigners, there were very few high-rises. But a
few blocks away was Huaihai Road, which had a couple of big
department stores, one of which had a Western supermarket in
its basement. With prices not much higher than at home, but
astronomically higher than at a regular Chinese market, one
could procure French cheeses, mesclun salad greens, and fresh
milk. To my delight, Shanghai's French past meant that baguettes
and cornichons were items in the import supply chain. These
were rarely touched by the locals, who complained about
crusts so tough they would pull out teeth and the rancid smell
of cheese (which, really, isn't much different than the smell of
stinky tofu), but there were enough foreigners in the city that

almost anything could be procured, for a price. And for those of us on missionary budgets, when an item reached its expiration date, it went on half price.

The price paid by foreigners, however, for going to the supermarket was that you had to pass through all the street vendors urging you, jostling you, to come see their watches, bags, or DVDs. We looked no different from any of the tourists who passed. One of the first phrases we used in our new home was *bu yao,* or "don't want,"

A couple of days after we were all settled in, my husband got a cryptic e-mail:

A friend told me you were new to town and needed some work. Let's meet for tea—Anthony

My husband wrote back and arranged to meet the man at a place nearby. He asked how we'd know who he was.

I'll be the one with the red rose in my lapel.

I thought he was joking, but then who knew. I felt like we were in a cloak-and-dagger novel by the time the day came to meet this unknown man. We went to the café, but as it turned out, we didn't need a rose to tell us who he was. There were only three foreigners in the place, and this guy looked like a Jehovah's Witness, even in his casual clothes. Many years later I found a picture of myself from those first days in Shanghai— a face puffy from humidity, the religious shine in my eyes, thinking I was blending in—and I was struck by how obvious I had looked. It was an ineffable thing, this religious sheen; even disguises and false premises couldn't hide it. The man introduced himself as Anthony, a fake name, for safety, he explained.

He was odd—China had a way of attracting the strange foreigners who didn't fit in at home—but he had been here for seven years already, and oddness seemed to be a quality that helped a person live so out of their element. He didn't tell us much about himself, other than that he was here with his wife, they were also from Canada, originally, and he had a Bible study to go to in half an hour. He got down to business. That is, how to be a Jehovah's Witness in a country where every facet of our worship and most ways we spent our time were illegal.

"Okay, guys, so the first rule is keep everything off the Internet, the phones, the texts. Take it as a given that any electronic device is being monitored. China has two million people monitoring the Internet."

I could tell he had given this speech before. How many times? How many of us were there here? Something in his bearing told me not to bother asking.

"Okay, got it," my husband said.

"We are Westerners, so we hold our meetings in hotels. There will be no Chinese people allowed at these meetings, and we call them parties. We get together for parties every Sunday. The location will be announced at the previous party. Never tell anyone the location of the next party except in person, and only if they have already been to our parties. We all pitch in to pay for the room, and we lock the doors so no staff can hear what is being said." He looked at the table to the right. "Do not tell your Bible students or other foreigners that we have meetings here. In fact, never reveal to any foreigner, no matter how safe they seem, that you are a Witness."

So there were meetings. But unlike home, where we were at the Kingdom Hall multiple times a week, we would see each other and study our materials only one day each week, and all the meetings were condensed into those few hours' time. Where did the Chinese meet? Were there any Chinese Witnesses? I knew not to ask.

"How do we dress? Are we supposed to dress up still?" At any Kingdom Hall, a man not in a suit and a woman not in a skirt below the knee would be counseled by the elders.

"Dress up, reasonably—business casual. The hotel staff thinks we are having a business meeting. Plus, this is still our worship to Jehovah so we dress accordingly."

Anthony took a drink of his tea and paused while a group of locals gathered their things to leave their table.

"Okay, I'm getting short on time here, but this is the deal. So we make friends. We don't preach. We approach people, we find out all we can about them before we ever bring up the Bible. When we bring up the Bible, we don't bring up Jehovah's Witnesses. They haven't heard of us anyway. Not important. What is important is that they, or anyone in their family, are not members of the Communist Party. Well, sort of. There are different kinds of party members. Some people just join because they need to get a job, like teachers. But vet them, ask them about themselves, see how they talk about the government. All it would take is for someone who knows we shouldn't be doing what we are doing to report us and it's over. Our cover is blown, and we are outed. Do not ruin it for the rest of us."

I still didn't really feel like I knew what to do, but that was it. Anthony gave us the address of the next meeting and shook our hands. "Any other questions?"

I couldn't think of any, because I didn't know what he would be allowed to answer.

"Oh, and don't ever pull out our literature unless it's covered with something," he went on. "Wrapping paper. Brown paper. You use the literature, of course, to study with them. Some brothers and sisters only let them borrow a copy, and don't even let them take a book home. Might be a good idea." He grabbed his bag and stood up. "Glad to have you. I'll see you on Sunday, then?" He reached for his wallet, but we insisted we'd pay, and he went on his way.

I widened my eyes at my husband, and he exhaled. Wow. So this was it. I felt a surge of emotion, which may have been religious in nature, or rooted in my love of strange new situations, hard to tell which. But to be able to serve God here in this land where our religion was banned—I felt proud, though I knew I shouldn't; pride was not a Christian quality. And although I was nervous after that speech, I couldn't wait to find my first Bible student. Most Witnesses were certain that the only reason Armageddon hadn't come yet was because the entire Earth had not yet been preached to—and China was one of the last frontiers (that is, of course, if you excluded the 1.8 billion Muslims in the world. But apparently, they wouldn't have a chance—and we didn't concern ourselves with that).

We walked out of the café and I registered as I did many times each day that there were, without exaggeration, thousands of people everywhere I went. Most were in a rush, I didn't even know how to say "Communist Party" in Chinese, and I worried that I would get someone in trouble.

What we had just learned was overwhelming, and shocking. First of all because they had sent us here relatively unprepared and unsupervised, which was unbelievable, given how far the tentacles of the organization reached into every other part of our lives, including our married sex life, not to mention our daily schedules. Our application process and training consisted of a letter to Hong Kong, a recommendation from our local elders, and a return letter that simply said "You are assigned to Shanghai, provide your contact information please and a brother will meet up with you on your arrival to explain all." That was it. This of course was a product of how secret the work was here; few Witnesses thought of going to preach in a place like China, and even fewer were permitted.

But further, it was shocking because the mandated life of a Witness in any country of the world is one of routine and structure. It is a trained, methodical, pious existence, where each week resembles the last, purposely, because this life you live is not "the real life." This life is a life in waiting. Meetings, preparation for those meetings, preaching, meeting in the evening, meeting the next morning. More preaching and study. Keeping oneself busy with work of a "spiritual" nature is considered a good way of staying out of trouble. Socializing is done with the same people you see at meetings, and involves spiritually fortifying, "upbuilding" talk, maybe a board game, or relating experiences you had while preaching. Your friends are those in your congregation, you work only enough to support yourself, and you never make friends outside your religious circle. The years of a Witness are spent in a life that does not flow but only ebbs in righteous monotony into its own reality, that does not proceed from conscious choices but rather in obedience, in neutral conversation, in not missing a meeting, in continual unquestioning study, and by turning in a report that proves your service was sufficient. One of the worst things one could be deemed is "irregular." Regularity is what breeds conformance, satisfaction, allegiance. And though rigorous, the constraints of this sort of life go largely unnoticed, mainly because humans are highly trainable creatures, and most of us have been doing this since we were children. It's the most natural life to someone who has been taught that this is the only way to live, and we are told that it is the best way of life, and we believe it. How would we know that anything could be different? What else would we do?

In China, suddenly, all of that was gone. We had been sanctioned, from the highest powers in the organization, to do the opposite. Don't meet often. Don't preach openly. Make friends. Worldly friends. Don't preach to them for a long, long time. Talk with them about things other than the Bible. And further—no territory cards carefully laying out the day's work, no gatherings for preaching. You walk out your front door and have to decide for yourself what you are going to do with your day.

I didn't even have to use my own name. It was as if I could be a different person.

In one of the most restrictive countries in the world, everything felt wide open. It was the first time my religion had granted me some space. We had Watchtower-sanctioned freedom. My passport buffered me from any dangers I may have faced in being a lawbreaker, giving me the subconscious luxury of birthplace. I was a holy outlaw, and one who now had a reason to join the life that was out there. My religion had opened a door I didn't know existed for us, God's people. Finding worldly friends, missing the meetings, lying about who I was, even hiding from the police were the right things to do. The amount of time freed up by the mere elimination of a few weekly congregation meetings left vast swaths of space to fill.

It was disorienting, yet my beliefs were what held it all in place—the truth. We were in the truth, and that was why we were here. Why I spoke Chinese. Why I had the truth that would set these people free.

I already knew I would never go back to preaching in Canada. I said a quick prayer of thanks to Jehovah for bringing me here and knew I was never going to leave, at least not until Armageddon. After that, I wanted to live by the ocean in a beautiful log home in the paradise.

I wasn't afraid. I was thrilled.

Now that we had our instructions, the next morning, my husband and I went out to "preach." It was strange not to meet up first with any other brothers or sisters, not to go out as a group, as we had for our whole lives. We simply walked out of the house the next day and thought about how we could strike up conversations with people.

It took some guts, and creativity, since we had been carried along by the scheduled infrastructure of our lives for so long, and at first we felt like we were floundering. But in some ways, this version of preaching was easier than it sounded, because many of the Chinese people we met were kind of floored by the fact that a foreigner was speaking Chinese to them, and most often they tried to stop and listen to what we were saying.

Of course, the problem was that things became more difficult if you wanted to take the conversation further than the initial pleasantries about your Chinese accent and the famous Canadian Da Shan. "Slipping in the Bible" is a clumsy proposition in the best of times—in a culture of people who have mostly never seen a Bible, or thought about reading one, it's not something that your conversation naturally veers toward. Furthermore, you couldn't really talk about the Bible to anyone you were actually close to, or comfortable with, as in, located within your circle of living—your workplace, your neighborhood—because if they knew your full name or address, then they'd be able to turn you in if they wanted to. That meant you had to find total strangers to just walk up to and make friends with, with the secret aim of converting them, or telling them why their culture and sets of beliefs, which originated thousands of years before your own, were inferior to your own—false, even—and should be tossed aside in favor of this.

This didn't strike me at the time as odd, possibly because when I was preaching in the West, I rarely met someone who was open enough to consider my beliefs, let alone accept them as superior to their own. People were not interested in discussing religion, and they thought that Witnesses coming to their door were an irritation to be put up with, at best. Thus, despite my diligent efforts over the fifteen years I had been preaching, I had only had a few Bible students, and had never converted any of them. Even so, I knew that my explanations of the world made more sense than anything else I had come across, if only I could find someone who had the right heart and would listen. I was as confident in my mission as a suicide bomber is of his: God would help me, and one day I would be in paradise for having done it.

The best idea we could come up with was to start by "fishing," as we called it, in stores. We knew of a large bookstore near People's Park, so we hopped on the bikes we had purchased and decided to go in that direction. We pulled out of our side street and rode up to the bike lane on Fuxing Road. China had a bike lane network far superior to that of Taiwan, with some streets designated as one-way, certain turns restricted, and police to enforce the bike traffic rules. The trees of Fuxing Road took us past Xintiandi, a newly restored group of hutong alley houses with luxury jewelry shops, designer clothing stores, and fancy bars with caviar on the menu, its cobblestones so perfect and clean they, too, seemed like goods laid out for the rich. From there, we made a sharp turn in the direction of the park.

We found a place to leave our bikes and locked their tires to their frames like everyone else did. Seeing as there were so many bikes, that was all it took to deter a thief, for the most part. I grabbed my bag from the bike basket. Normally, in any other preaching territory, I'd have filled the bag with books and magazines to give to people, and a Bible. But my load was light today: just a wallet, a notebook, and some tissues. I wasn't sure yet when we could actually give people literature to read, but certainly it wouldn't be for a while. I didn't know if people ever got searched.

My husband and I thought it would probably make it harder to talk to other people if we were together, so we decided to split up in the park before trying the bookstore. I'd look for women, he'd look for men.

I found a bench in a leafy enclave and sat down to observe. I was still quite unfamiliar with the culture here. From my encounters thus far, people seemed very different from their counterparts in Taiwan. There was an intensity in the

Mainlanders—in the hardness of their accent, in their single-mindedness of purpose—that I hadn't noticed in Taiwan, where the people were for the most part very friendly and open to foreigners. Everywhere a foreigner went in Taiwan, no matter what their looks, people would tell them as a form of greeting: "You're so beautiful" or "You're so handsome." Here, most people noticed you, registered you were a foreigner, but then looked away. After about a month without compliments, I became vain, wondering if the pollution had ruined any good looks I might have had across the strait.

Shanghai was also a much bigger city than Taipei, and while that was no doubt a contributing factor to the general feeling of coolness the people gave off, the fifty years and body of water that separated them had created very different societies. The citizens who had fled to Taiwan in 1949 after Mao's victory had been sheltered from the events that barraged the Mainland after the Communist government took over. But those left on the Mainland had lived through terrible famines, constant political upheaval, a revolution that led to forced relocations and losses of community, a shattering of institutions, a ransacking of homes, imprisonments, and the systematic murder of many intellectuals and professionals.

Shanghai in particular had been a stage for some of the many harrowing experiences of the Cultural Revolution in the 1960s and 1970s. Many of the people I was looking at had lived through it, participated in it, or been victims of those times. With Mao's encouragement, one million Red Guards had marched through the park I was sitting in now, in an audacious attempt to oust the mayor.

Bit by bit, I would come to know the stories of some of these people, but for now, sitting in the park, they seemed to be an impenetrable mass. What I knew of their language did not give me intimacy past the odd sharp shove in the back I received while exiting a subway car.

I smiled at two women walking by, and one of them smiled back. Despite the thousands of hours of my life that I had spent preaching, I really had no idea how to do this, and I was feeling timid. But there was no not doing it—I needed to catch up on my hours, as I had to do seventy hours of preaching per month, and I'd already been stuck a week waiting for permission to go out and talk to people. At home we couldn't start counting our time until we called on someone. I decided that in China, a smile at a stranger could count.

I had also never really been on my own before to preach. Even when we went door-to-door back home, we'd always go in twos. My whole life was lived in the presence of brothers and sisters. I rarely had time alone at home or in Taiwan; there was always a preaching group to get to, a meeting to attend, a family study to be had, or a congregation event to go to. I felt small and vulnerable. I was one of twenty million people, and I felt my perspective skewing to adjust to my new position as I looked out from that park bench.

After a while, mosquitoes started biting my legs, and the humidity felt like a paste on my skin, so I crossed the street and walked down to the giant Foreign Languages bookstore on FuZhou Road. Since my Chinese was relatively fluent, but not yet fluent enough to understand everything that was said, I thought it might be a good place to find Chinese people who could also speak a little English. Reducing the number of people in my field of vision might help my confidence levels, too, and maybe I could find an English-Chinese dictionary to look up the word for "Communist Party."

The bookstore felt like a department store. It was multistoried, immense, and crammed with people. Most of the patrons were young, probably students and professionals in their twenties and thirties who had a bit of money to spare. If I had thought the number of people might seem smaller in a store, I was wrong—the ratio of people to me felt even larger in here. I decided to take a walk around first, to get a feel for the place, and to people-watch awhile, to get a sense of this demographic.

I first browsed in the English Classics section and made a mental note to come back here for books when things settled down, since they were the only English-language novels I saw that were cheap; many of the rest were imported. There weren't many Chinese people in this section, so I took the staircase that was square in the center of the building and went up to the third floor to see the other departments. I settled on the section that had textbooks for learning the English language. It seemed like a place where a foreigner might be expected to hang out, and Chinese teachers might be interested in the books, too. I looked around for security cameras. Even though the store was really crowded, I felt like I stood out, a tall white woman among the leveled-off, uniform masses of Saturday shoppers.

I opened an English teaching textbook and kept watch, glancing over the top of the book. I was nervous. I was used to doorbells and sermons. Plus, my Chinese was still limited to some degree. I didn't know how I'd fare in a conversation, given that I was getting used to the accents here. I said a prayer, to summon up some boldness. Jehovah did not help me talk to anyone for the next twenty minutes, but finally a woman in her late twenties with wire-rimmed glasses stopped at the shelf beside me. She wore a tight mohair sweater and plaid wool pants. Her everyday plainness was just enough to make her feel approachable.

"*Ni hao*," I said, self-consciously.

A large smile broke out on her face. "You speak Chinese!" she said.

"*Bu tai hao.*" (That meant "Not too well.")

"*Waaa, tai hao le!*" ("Wow, this is incredible!")

We chatted for a few minutes, and then much to her surprise, I asked her if we could stay in touch. We exchanged phone numbers and promised to get together soon. I found out she was not a teacher but a young woman from Jiangsu Province who had moved to Shanghai for work. She worked in an office, but her passion was learning English. She had taught herself, in her small town, and after graduating from university had moved on her own to Shanghai. That was a few years ago. She was by herself here; all her family was back in her hometown and had never even been here for a visit.

Jean seemed quite shy and maybe a little naive, yet the few minutes I had heard of her life story already told me she had guts. And that I wasn't the only one who had come to this city and started over. There were lots of us. Shanghai was one place in China where reinvention was possible, even for a Chinese person from a very traditional family. It was modern, anonymous, and full of things and people and concepts that would be unheard-of in their home cities or the countryside. In spite of all its seeming constraints and government control, arrival in Shanghai was probably the closest thing Jean and I had ever felt to freedom.

I didn't try to speak to anyone else the rest of the morning; somehow managing one conversation felt like enough, given the amount of energy I mustered to do it, and the satisfaction it delivered. I had "preached" to my first local. I texted my husband, and we met to go for noodles.

My husband and I were far from the first missionaries who had come to China, enjoying noodles while hiding our purpose, determined to convert the Chinese to our way of living. Nor were we the first group to be banned.

The first recorded Christian missionaries went to China in 635 CE, and when they got as far as Xian they set up their houses of worship. However, early on it became evident to the emperors of the day that Westerners had not only a different way of worshipping heaven but also a form of hierarchy that excluded them from the chain of command. This, they decided, meant that it was a religion that did not suit the Chinese.

Thus, the Qing dynasty emperor Yongzheng made a proclamation:

In the empire we have a temple for honoring Heaven and sacrificing to Him. The first day of every year we burn incense and paper to honor Heaven. We Manchus have our own particular rites for honoring Heaven; the Mon-

gols, Chinese, Russians, and Europeans also have their
own particular rites for honoring Heaven. [E]veryone has
his way of doing it. As a Manchu, Urcen should do it
like us.

Shortly thereafter, the tentative hospitality of the Chinese
went cold, and in 845 CE, Emperor Wuzong banned all of
Christianity, with any Christian assets in China being forfeited
to the state. Then began a long period where there were no
Christians, and no conversions.

But China would not stay sequestered from the tenacious
missionaries forever. Emperors came and went, and the Christians remained. As travel became easier and interactions with
foreign governments increased in the nineteenth and twentieth
centuries, lofty Western-style buildings came to Shanghai's
Bund, trade and travel routes brought people back and forth,
and the missionaries came once again, driven by their calling
to "save" the Chinese from their own culture and beliefs. By
the time I arrived, in 2005, to be a Christian in China was the
opposite of what it was to be a Christian in my home country—
it was cool.

Part of the reason for this may have been the complete
spiritual vacuum the postrevolution years of Communism had
created in China. Any belief other than that sanctioned by the
government had been forbidden for decades. And by the 1990s,
as the country opened up, the government had relaxed its hold
on people's inner lives. Though now three official Christian
"churches" were recognized by the government, they operated
under strict regulation, and any other Christian sect had to

conduct its activities secretly, underground. Becoming a Christian had been a modern, reactionary move for many young people.

And while people's lives were getting better in many ways economically, this also created a void, because life was now less of a struggle. There were gaps in morality—milk distributors watering down milk and hiding their act by thickening it with melamine so they could make more money, killing babies in the process. Videos were shown on the news of incidents of apathy and cruelty—a woman being hit by a car and lying injured on the ground, the other cars just driving around her until a large truck finally put her out of her misery by driving over her.

But beyond that, there is of course no better way to make something cool than to make it forbidden and mysterious. It was difficult to get information about the Bible on the Mainland, or about Christianity, because the Internet is censored. Christianity was also a way into friendships with foreigners, because there was no foreigner more interested in the people of their host country than a foreigner with the drive to convert. And many of the Chinese whom I met had an intense curiosity about Westerners. To them, a Christian in their midst was a window into a world they had never entered, and a chance to understand something that had been closed off to them. For others, it was a way to rebel from their traditional parents. Many of the Chinese Bible students I had would generously compare me to a Western movie star. It was as if we were all celebrities in that era, even the most nerdy among us.

My first glimpse into the world of modern-day Christianity

in China came after I had been there for quite some months. I discovered that there were other people like us, preaching underground, when one of my Bible students told me that she had been lured to another Christian meeting in someone's home by a local who had given her our Jehovah's Witness magazines. She told me they had said that Jesus had returned for his second coming in the form of a Chinese woman from Shandong province. Though they weren't Witnesses themselves, they were using our literature as bait, since they didn't have any means to print books on their own. To get spirituality-hungry people to come to the meetings they held in their homes, they figured that flashing any old Bible publication would work. When I did some research on the group, I found stories about people who had converted and been baptized into the faith and later tried to leave, but they were physically restrained from doing so. There were reports of beatings, and even killings. One disillusioned friend of my student knew a woman who, when she tried to disassociate herself from the group, had her leg broken after a beating.

The next day, before I could figure out what the next step in my preaching might look like, I got a text from Jean:

I would like to invite you for a dinner. Please come to my house Saturday?

I accepted gratefully and promised to come. She sent me detailed directions about how to get to her apartment by subway. Take Line 3 to Caoxi Station. When you see the IKEA, you know you're getting close; take a sharp right.

Come Saturday, I climbed the staircase to her apartment, a bottle of juice and a box of chocolates I had brought from home in hand, and passed the other residents cooking their dinners in the shared kitchens at the end of each open-air hallway. I got to Jean's door and knocked.

"*Ni hao*," Jean said excitedly, swinging the metal grate open.

There were two beds arranged in an L-shape in the room. Her roommate stood formally next to the one with a pink ruffled bedspread. Between the beds was a table on which food was already served. Four dishes: sautéed vegetables, light green soybeans with peppers, meat in a sauce, fried tofu, and of course rice in the rice cooker.

"*Huanying. Qing jin!*" ("Welcome. Come in!") Jean's roommate smiled, her eyes crinkling at their corners.

Jean rinsed off chopsticks and bowls in the sink next to the bathroom and brought them to the table wet.

"I hope you like it. I am concerned it's not too delicious."

Jean opened up the lid of the digital rice cooker and scooped rice into each of our bowls.

"*Chi fan!*" ("Eat!")

She motioned to the platters, then took up her chopsticks and placed a chunk of meat in my bowl, then some leafy greens. She urged me to eat. I wanted to wait for her, but she insisted.

The roommate watched as I took a bite.

"*Hao chi!*" I said enthusiastically. What I lacked in vocabulary I tried to make up for with tone of voice.

Jean clapped a little and laughed, then insisted, shaking her head, "*Bu hao chi!*" ("It tastes terrible!")

"No! It's delicious," I insisted. She really was a good cook.

We chatted in half-broken Chinese, half-broken English as we ate. Jean's English was good, better than my Chinese; she was the envy of her roommate, who seemed to understand much of what we said, yet was too shy to join in. Jean studied all the time and had been the only kid in her village in northern Jiangsu who could speak English. Her older cousin would bring her books when he returned from his business trips to Tianjin. A few years ago, Jean had moved to Shanghai for work, and found a job as a receptionist at a real estate company. Every month, she would send part of her salary back to her parents. In spite of the one-child policy, her parents had managed to have six children (five girls and a boy) by dodging the authorities. One of the girls was adopted; the family moved around a lot to avoid fines or sterilization. They stopped having children after they had a boy.

Jean liked her job because the boss was an Englishman, and she sometimes got up the courage to practice speaking English with him. She related stories of their mundane conversations about dinner or haircuts with delight. She made 1,800 renminbi a month, equivalent to about $280.

I tried to casually return the conversation to Jean's family.

"So . . . what does your father do for a living in Jiangsu?"

"He's a farmer."

This seemed safe. Or were the farmers Communist Party members? After all, didn't they have to give a percentage of their crops to the state? I tried to think back to the Chinese movies I had seen, my only reference.

"What about your mom?"

"She looks after the kids and my grandmother, mostly. Sometimes she helps with the farming or makes crafts to sell." Oh, right, and they had six children—surely they couldn't be that Communist.

"And your brothers and sisters, do any of them work?"

"My younger sister is in school, my older sister has a baby. Though my brother is in the army."

Army. Why hadn't Anthony mentioned anything about the army? This seemed like a major alarm bell. If you were in the army, you must be a Communist.

"But he has been writing my parents from the camp, telling them he wants to be a pop music star. They are very upset. But he asked me all the time, so I saved money and sent him a guitar at his birthday. Here is a photo of him playing." She flipped open her cell phone. His lazy teenage posture reassured me somewhat as to his level of devotion to the chairman.

We finished eating, and Jean refused to let me help her clear the plates. "Sit, sit," she kept ordering me, physically restraining me with one arm.

As I sat on the bed, waiting for her to return, I noticed the wardrobe had only a pair or two of pants in it, and one dress.

I stayed for a while after the meal, eventually excusing myself and making a plan with Jean to meet up again next week. I needed to find out a lot more about her before we got to the point where I could preach to her.

The secret meeting Anthony had given us the instructions to attend was at 1:00 p.m. on Sunday, in a hotel at the far end of Huaihai Road. My husband and I got ready in the morning, dressing like we would have for a meeting at home. We had photocopied *Watchtower*s for this week's meeting in Taiwan and brought them with us, and I rolled mine up and pushed them to the bottom of my purse. I had already wrapped my Bible, as if it were a gift, in brown paper, to make it less obvious. I shoved a scarf on top not only to keep everything covered but also in case the air-conditioning at the hotel was too strong, as it often was in public buildings in China.

I turned off our air conditioner, pulled the heavy metal door closed behind me, and we went down to the courtyard. Our neighbor looked at us from the corner of her eye as we tromped down the staircase, the particular clomp of my heels something unusual for a Sunday early afternoon. I said *"Ni hao"* as I passed, but her pots were clanging and she didn't seem to hear. I supposed it was better to keep a low profile anyway.

We walked to the main road and waited at the corner. In our formal attire, we stood out even more than usual. This made me nervous, so I raised my arm to wave down a cab as quickly as I could. The first taxi that saw us stopped, and we climbed into the smooth cloth seats, both of us in the back.

To be safe, my husband had painstakingly written the address in Chinese on a piece of paper so that we could be sure we wouldn't say a tone wrong and end up at an entirely different place. The taxi driver took the paper, nodded in understanding, and pressed the accelerator down hard.

We whizzed through the streets that were never empty, even on a Sunday, the driver beeping his horn like a nervous tic, even when no one was in his way. I said a few words to him, asked him where he was from, told him where we were from, then my husband and I chatted with each other about the things we always talked about: our failed attempts at meeting people, funny things that had happened, the things we had learned in Chinese. We were like any other Witness couple in some ways; we all received the same marriage advice and tried to apply it. But from the outset I had known it had been a mistake for us to get married.

I had harbored this gut-sinking feeling since the day before our wedding, a feeling all the more overwhelming because in a godly marriage, there was no allowance for divorce. My grandma had told me once that marriage was like bobbing for apples: you never really knew which kind you had until you had already bit in. And it wasn't that my husband was the rotten apple—I was the one who had a rotting inside. It had started before we even met.

He was twenty-one and I was twenty-two the first time he walked into the Kingdom Hall I attended, there visiting a friend who was in the same congregation as me. He was tall and had curly brown hair, and had not yet lost the disproportionately skinny and long arms and legs of puberty. I found him handsome and sweet. We had a prolonged engagement of eleven months consisting of controlled libido and harrowing blue balls.

He was a virgin and I was not. My situation was unusual. It was uncommon in our religion for a person to go into marriage sexually experienced, because we were required to wait until after we were married to do anything more than kiss or hold hands. The Bible and our organization strictly prohibited premarital sex and any form of immorality. Those who didn't wait faced consequences, one of which involved confessing in detail before a panel of three men to what immoral thing it was you had done. After you confessed, the men would confer about your case as you waited in the other room, deciding among themselves whether you were repentant enough. If they decided you weren't, a sentence that involved being kicked out of the organization until such time that they decided you could be let back in was proclaimed and announced to the congregation, so that all your family and friends knew to shun you. This was called "disfellowshipping."

After being disfellowshipped, you sat in the back row at the meetings, ignored by all, penitent for a number of months or years. Then, if you had been living a moral life for that time period, you could apply for reinstatement. But in the interim, you were treated as though you were dead. If someone you knew passed you on the street, they were to look the other way. This was not a small punishment for people who have built their entire lives inside such a closed group.

I was sixteen when I first saw Thomas, the man with whom I would have sex before marriage. Thomas was five years older than me. His family had moved into my congregation, and I became best friends with his younger sister, Lina, a kindred soul who loved poetry and slept late. As we became closer friends, I started spending nights over at her house, as teenage girls do. Thomas, of course, was there, and began flirting with me over grapefruit juice at breakfast, and in the kitchen at night, when by some chance we were alone for a second as the family members took their turns brushing their teeth in the one bathroom. I didn't even really know what flirting was, or how to do it, but it came easily to me with this man around, this man who smelled so good, who had graduated from high school and had a job, who played music like "Free Fallin' " loud in his car, who drank beers with his dad, and who slept on a giant waterbed that smelled of Giorgio VIP cologne in the basement of their family home. He was smart, intense, and the first Witness I had met who was interested in books like I was—except he knew more.

Lina and I usually had hung out by ourselves, but now her brother often joined us. We spent more and more time together, every chance we could, but rarely alone, because two people of the opposite sex were told not to spend time together without a chaperone present. The young people in the congregation did a lot of socializing, so there was always a way to hang out in a group.

Thomas had a harder time being a Witness than I did. Years later, when I ran into him in Vancouver on one of my visits home and spent an evening with him catching up— I was thirty-three and he was almost forty—I was shocked to discover I was the one who had left the religion and he hadn't. Of all the people who should have left, it was he. I wondered how it was that way back then we could have played cribbage all afternoon in only our robes, had sex in an outhouse on a road trip to the desert, talked about books, and gone to nude painting classes, yet not once have ever considered investigating whether our religion was false. The grips of being raised a Witness and the consequences of losing our entire world and family had their hold on us—had consequences that could hijack all the things that we loved, including each other.

The first time we kissed, outside my family home, was one night after I had been hanging out with his sister and he offered to drive me home, before anyone suspected that we had feelings for each other. On the ride up the hill, whenever he shifted the gears, he touched the corner of my hand with his. I never knew anything could feel so electric. As he turned onto my street, he was blasting the Rolling Stones with our windows down. He pulled his brown Honda hatchback up beside the bushes that stood like sentries around my house, and when I got out, he did, too. After talking a minute, he grabbed me and kissed me, just out of sight of any parents who might have happened to look out the front window. The sentries were our allies, Mick Jagger reminding us that "You Can't Always Get What You Want," through the still summer suburban air.

There was much that we could not get that we wanted. I went into the house, exhilarated and petrified.

I knew if my dad found out, I would never be allowed at Lina and Thomas's house again. But when I walked in the door, my heart pounding, I knew I was safe, for now—the main floor was dark, my mom was in bed, and I heard the TV from below, which signified that my dad was down there, drunk, and not coming out.

His drinking had become much worse since he had quit his job and moved us all out west for a fresh start—the point of which was to get my sister away from her worldly friends. He was going to take a few months off, then get another job. But instead, he took up full-time drinking. He now stayed down in the TV room all day and night, and I barely saw him, except drunk—once, he emerged naked after spilling wine all over his robe; another time I heard him in the foyer putting on his shoes and getting his keys. I realized instantly that he was going out to the car, and I was terrified, but more terrified that he would kill someone while driving intoxicated. I willed myself out of my room and told him that I didn't think he should be driving. He told me to go back to my room, where I waited, blaming myself for the person he might kill. He came back forty minutes later and went back down to his TV, box of wine from the liquor store in its brown paper bag.

Of course, I never told anyone any of this, drunkenness being a disfellowshipping offense, and it was too scary to contemplate what it would mean if anyone in the congregation knew.

After that night of the first kiss, at any opportunity, Thomas and I would grab each other and we would kiss deeply—since kissing was the one intimate act that did not require a confession to the elders, you did it deeply, and often. I was terrified of getting caught, but Thomas was totally relaxed as we made out in different parts of his house when no one was looking. This was no small feat in a family that had six children and two parents. But no one suspected, because my visits to Lina's house seemed innocent: a girl hanging out with her friend. I had been auxiliary pioneering over the summer—going out in service fifty hours a month—and I was so good and so zealous no one would suspect I would be surreptitiously kissing Thomas. I probably surprised myself most of all.

And yet I couldn't stop. I knew that dating at my age was wrong, and kissing someone was considered "courtship," only to be undertaken with a view to marriage shortly thereafter. I wasn't ready to get married—most Witnesses waited until they were eighteen for that. But if we could just keep it to kissing, everything would be fine. That wasn't immoral, right?

A few months later, I was in Thomas's car alone again, by some lucky chance, driving home from a get-together, I think, and the friend who had come with us had left early. It was dark in the car, and as we drove up his long, curvy street, Thomas slowed down to a crawl and took my hand. He pulled it over to his lap and placed it atop his pants, over his hard penis.

I felt frozen. No one had ever told me that a penis could do such a thing. How did something that I had only seen limply dangling like a dead mouse—in the swimming pool change rooms I had been in as a child—transform itself into something ten, twenty times its size? Or what was the math here, a hundred times? I knew this crossed every line, this was bad. Bad. Bad. But I was in shock. And I would do anything Thomas wanted to; he seemed to know what he was doing in life, and I was completely unsure at all times.

I shifted my hand, tentatively. My anxiety over wondering what it was I was supposed to do was louder than any feelings of revulsion or doom at having crossed some line that I knew would lead me to some kind of downfall. Those thoughts just sat, quieted by the hypnotic effect of something so forbidden. It wasn't like I had no idea what sex was, but my parents had never explained anything specific about it to me. All I really knew was what I heard from the platform at the meetings, which was that sex or anything related to it was "wrongdoing." The very significant gaps in my knowledge were filled in sparsely with a health sciences book my friend had found in a library, requisite fare for any two giggling girls in junior high. But there are no illustrations of hard-ons in junior high school libraries. The actual logistics of how that thing that peed managed to get into a woman's vagina had never been fully contemplated by me before. This immorality was an anatomy lesson for me, inscrutable things revealed in the darkness of a brown Honda Civic.

And as I sat here now, in the seat of his car, my hand having become something that no longer belonged to me, I felt no eroticism, no desire; this man who was so attractive to me, so delectable, whose pillow I would hold and smell when his sister was in the bathroom, whom I could not sleep at night for thinking about, the touch of whose hand would make my vagina, such as it was, seeing as I had not contemplated my own body parts much, trickle. I was sitting, stunned, hand pressed against this leaden object. I did not know what happened next in the black night of the car's interior, because I did not know what was supposed to happen.

Thomas had stopped the car now, we were just a few doors away from his house, and he was leaned back in a kind of ec-stasy, far away from me, his foot on the brake, its light shining red on the hedges. All went still. He returned my hand to my lap and held it for a moment.

It was getting late and I was worried about what had just happened and whether his mom would come out and see us like this, so I told him I had to go. He reached over and hugged me, and that felt good, but my thoughts had already begun to race about what this meant, and what I had done.

Thomas did not seem worried as he gave me a long kiss. I loved kissing him and yet already wished none of it had happened—the grapefruit juice, the smelling of pillows. I had just committed the gravest sin of my life. And this would mean everything between me and Thomas was going to come crash-ing down, and even worse, ruin our relationship with Jehovah.

Thomas wasn't thinking about this though. At least he had his afterglow to buy him some time. I had never been much fascinated by the idea of committing a sin, but I was surprised it wasn't more enjoyable than this. In shock, I walked the few blocks to my house.

I was the kind of person who preferred to obey God's laws and not to sin, rather than sin and take advantage of God's grand forgiveness. Especially because that forgiveness could only come with three men as an intermediary. From childhood on, my inner world was the one thing no one could touch in a house that felt at times quietly chaotic under the unspoken problem of my father's drinking. The only other figure I had to rely on was a mother who was distant and seemed to love me less than other mothers loved their daughters, which meant no falling back on anyone. But I had found that by following all the rules and living as a good girl, I could function. Living meant flying under the radar and keeping the chaos at bay.

Thomas, on the other hand, was one for living now and repenting later, and though he believed as much as I did that we had the truth, he was prone to pushing the boundaries of what we were permitted to do as Witnesses, then repenting it later. A liaison with someone like him was tantalizing and thrilling for a person like me, who had lived so little. But I was deeply uncomfortable the next day when Thomas called and said we had to go to the elders. I knew that there was no alternative; God had seen what we had done, and confession was the only way to forgiveness. But still, I felt breached in some way, our privacy shattered. How could all of these feelings of love produce this as their result? It wasn't that I regretted what had happened so much—I didn't really understand very clearly what had happened—but I was someone who never even told my parents things about my life. What did these men have to do with it? I was scared.

An appointment was made for us to each talk to an elder separately; this was the protocol for a first offense. After we explained that we hadn't actually had sex, it was deemed appropriate by the elders that we each confess what had happened, receive some counsel, and be reminded of what the scriptures said about such abhorrent conduct. Though I had not wanted to touch Thomas's penis, and had no interest in touching penises in general, I felt terribly guilty. I was willing to go through this process because I knew that hiding sin led you to bloodguilt—and Jehovah had seen it all. I could not sit in the Kingdom Hall knowing that Jehovah knew what I had done and hide it from the congregation. That would make the sin infinitely worse.

A few days later, I met with Brother Davies. He seemed a little uncomfortable himself and not at all ironic when he asked me about "the incident at hand." He was an older brother who was legally blind; his cloudy retinas gave a coating of dignity to the occasion. I explained that I had touched Thomas's "private part," grateful that eye contact was not necessary. He asked me how long I had touched it. I couldn't remember. Had I rubbed it? I said I wasn't sure. He asked, "Did he climax?" I had no idea what he was asking me. I started to cry. I felt so bad, my innocence as a human being and my goodness before Jehovah forever marred by this incident. The brother said we could stop there. He would discuss with the brothers whether they needed to form a judicial committee and then get back to me. He also said I had to tell my parents.

I didn't. I didn't tell my parents anything, ever. Even a command from God's mouthpiece himself, here in front of me, couldn't override the extreme discomfort I felt in revealing such intimate, personal things to them; that was not how our family worked. I lived in fear that the elders would tell my father, and that worst of all, my parents would not allow me to spend time with Thomas and his family anymore. Part of what

I loved about Thomas was his family. The kids would come home at night and their parents would put on the tea and they'd all sit around the kitchen table, sometimes until past midnight, listening to stories from their parents' wild days before they had come into the truth. His mom had been a Catholic nun and his dad a rebellious musician in a leather jacket, playing in a band. They were a total mismatch in personality, but they had had child after child in a very Catholic fashion, even though they had converted to be Jehovah's Witnesses shortly after they were married and as such were allowed to use birth control. But despite their parents' conflicts and their relative lack of money, their home felt happier than mine. They all piled into the family car and did fun outings together on Saturdays after service. They had movie nights together each Friday and ate pizza and junk food, the mom muting with the remote anytime there was vulgar language or a sex scene. The adult children liked to hang around, even after they had moved out.

And they invited me along. His mom had a nickname for me. This was very different from the atmosphere in my home, and it was the first of many relationships where I felt as attached to the family of someone I dated as I did to the person I was dating. I longed to be a part of a family, to be somewhere with love. Thomas was all of this to me, and as such there was no way I could give him up, once I had found it.

The elders never told my parents, and though I had an overly sensitive conscience when it came to the rules and regulations of my faith, I justified myself in not telling them, because I had done the hardest thing and told the elders. Jehovah knew I was repentant, and that was what mattered. Perhaps having a drunk dad gave you some leeway for these matters in God's eyes? Luckily, the elder I had spoken to was kind and said that I would not have to appear before the three brothers in a judicial committee, therefore there was no danger of a public announcement that I was reproved or had done some-thing unclean. He advised that I not see Thomas anymore, es-pecially alone, and that I spend more time studying the Bible and the publications.

I was done with "heavy petting," as they called it, after that. But I was not done with Thomas. Which meant I wasn't actu-ally done with heavy petting. The next two years turned into a protracted, on-and-off foreplay of sorts. We tried to stay away from each other, to be chaste and good, but we couldn't. I fin-ished high school and we both moved out of our homes, and the newfound autonomy we felt in our changed circumstances, in the rich thrill of nascent adulthood, wasn't suited to self-control. Finally, one afternoon in the summer we had sex on a bed in his apartment in the West End of Vancouver, where the mattress touched all four walls of the room and a breeze blew the curtain, periodically darkening the room, then brightening it with swells of light.

After we confessed, we were swiftly disfellowshipped—kicked out of the congregation—for what we had done. But I had what felt like love, for a while. And then it rotted me. None of the apples would ever taste right now.

After the elders in our new congregations disfellowshipped Thomas and me, the first thing he did was buy some cigars. I was surprised by this—why this?—but tried a few puffs. They weren't celebratory, it was more that we smoked them because we could now. Later we realized cigarettes were much better, and for something to do, we would drive an hour to the U.S. border and buy beer and Camels and smoke them on the way back home, windows open. All the things that were forbidden were suddenly available to us—if we were bad enough to have sex, well, we were bad enough to smoke or try getting drunk. Our reasoning was: What was the difference at this point?

Like people on a trip, we were enamored with this new place, we saw none of its flaws, we thought it was better than where we had lived. But the sparkle of it all couldn't block out everything else for long. Armageddon came to mind more and more frequently. Though we had been put outside the organization, we believed it was the truth as strongly as we had when we were on the inside, and soon we began to feel guilty. We knew Jehovah could see us, even if the elders or our parents had no idea what we were doing. It was one thing to sin and flagellate oneself for it, but we were rather enjoying it, which seemed sort of unconscionable.

Also, our families would not speak to us. For Thomas this was more difficult than for me, as my mother was already not speaking to me since I had moved out of our home, I think mainly because she could not forgive me for not taking her side when I was sixteen and she decided to leave my dad. She had asked my sister and me to write letters to the court, saying that we did not want our dad to have custody of us and our little brother. I wasn't taking my dad's side either, given the state he was in, but still I refused to write the letter because I knew how much it would hurt him. My sister complied, and I was in the car with my dad when he got her letter from the lawyer and read it, crying. As his eyes dripped, I felt porous and helpless. The world seemed to lose its shape. Now my dad was living at his own mother's apartment, drinking with her, smelling up her rooms with sweat and unwashed pants as he had ours, and I did not want to talk to him.

Two years after this letter, sick from years of alcoholism, my father's kidneys shut down, and after a sudden, and grotesque, six weeks of his body slowly poisoning itself, he died. I was only eighteen and had never considered that death could be the outcome of those hours spent drinking and TV watching, but I suppose there is no ceremonious end when that becomes your life. He was shocked himself, and as he lay dying, he kept trying desperately to get out of the hospital bed, saying he would take me on a road trip. He was forty-seven. The only person in his life who had ever asked him to stop drinking was me—I had written him a letter and left it on his dresser when I was fourteen. He had taken me into the TV room after reading it, the sour air filling the awkward silence between a parent and the child who has become the parent, and asked me if my mother had put me up to this. I told him no. Did members of other families ever talk to each other about the fact that there was a passed-out man in their basement? I thought to myself. My dad cried in front of me—the only other time I had seen him cry—and stopped drinking for a week. Then he started again.

On the day of my father's funeral, I sat in the back row of the Kingdom Hall, because that was where disfellowshipped people were allowed to sit. No one spoke to me. No one even looked at me.

After the funeral, Thomas and I knew we couldn't go on like this; while we were fornicating, oblivious to all, my father had been dying, the world had been going crazy, a riot had broken out in our city, and we saw prophecies of the last days being fulfilled everywhere we looked. Our everlasting destruction would be sealed should Jehovah's day of judgment arrive during our foray into hedonism. I wanted to see my dad again, in the resurrection. If I died at Armageddon, I would not live forever.

We had no choice. We broke up permanently, because though we had tried, and prayed, and agonized, and done trial separations, we simply could not stop having sex, and the only solution for having sex was to get married, but Thomas couldn't bring himself to marry. He had never wanted to be one of those typical Witnesses who married young and lived unhappily trapped, like my parents, and his. I, of course, would have been fine with it, over the alternative.

So we separated for good, finally, and I spent the greater part of the next year alone. When I say alone, I mean grievously alone, except for the meetings I went to where I sat in the back row, repentant. I suffered the loss of my dad, alone in my small apartment, sitting on the carpet sobbing many nights after work, where no one could hear me but my downstairs neighbor. I discovered that if I drank precisely four beers over the course of an evening, things would get more manageable (with a dim awareness that this had likely been my father's line of reasoning). During the day, I had a job as a secretary at a law firm, but I barely spoke to people at the office. Every night, every weekend, I saw no one except those I passed on the street or in a store. Sometimes by Monday morning I would have lost my voice, having not used it for so many hours. I wonder sometimes why I didn't make friends. But I was so trained to be wary of the world, even when I had been totally kicked out of the congregation and the world was all I had, when the world would have picked me up and taught me that all of this insanity was wrong, I still preemptively rejected it. I was afraid of it.

On my nineteenth birthday (the legal drinking age in British Columbia), I took the bus to a university campus not too far from my home. I had no one to celebrate this adult milestone with, so I sat in the bar in the student union on a carpeted cube seat and ordered a beer for myself for the first time. I sat drinking it, awkwardly, wishing I had not come, yet knowing that somehow this was an important day in my passage through life, one that should not be spent without the company of others, of one's peers. I was the same age as all of these people;

they had the same fresh skin and wore the same colored Champion sweatshirts I did. And yet, though I had been drawn to this bar of all bars, it never even occurred to me that I could go to school here, that I could do the things they did, that I was perhaps like them, in some ways.

Around two years passed from the time I was disfellowshipped until the elders agreed that I was repentant and clean enough in my conduct to be allowed back in. I was now twenty-one and had moved apartments, meaning I now lived in a different congregation's territorial boundaries. One of the elders went to the platform and made a simple announcement just after the meeting's intermission: "Amber Scorah has been reinstated." I was given a new start, a result of the forgiveness of my God and these three older men who had grilled me prior to making the announcement, to find out when was the last time I'd had sex. Now that the announcement had been made, people flocked around me at the end of the meeting, all shaking my hand and welcoming me back, prodigal daughter.

Just over a year later, I met my husband-to-be.

And this was how I came to be the rot of this marriage—I was already so full of nostalgia and infected with the knowledge of something different by the time I kissed my husband for the first time that it became indistinguishable to me, years later, whether it was desire for Thomas that had made me discontent, or the taste I'd had of who I had been with him. Thomas and I had lived in a paradise that didn't need destruction to create, that demanded nothing of anyone else, that did not need others to accept it. We danced to Roy Orbison in his living room and made coffee all day long. We'd share cold beer while we had conversations all night on the narrow balcony, our bodies perched half inside the apartment and half out. When Thomas found work as a city bus driver, I would go along with him every weekend on the routes he drove, sitting in the first seat, drinking extra-large coffees with cream all the way through the city and out over the highway to the beaches near the ferries. We'd make out in the back of the bus during his break, then sit, bashful, as he let the passengers on for the ride back to the city. This had felt like paradise to me.

I had chosen the paradise that would last forever, though. Plus, why couldn't I dance with my husband and drink Beck's? I could.

So it wasn't even Thomas, maybe. Or love. Maybe it was the taste of being myself that I sought. But not understanding who I was, or what the freedom to be one's self looked like, I mistook it for a man. The taste of who I was became intertwined with the taste of his mouth, his skin, his cum, because with him I had, for the first time, lived as myself. And it was therefore impossible to know that I was a unique individual, or to know where he began and my longings ended, or that I had agency and could choose my own life, and that life did not exist only with him. Because any act of self-discovery was hemmed in by the rules I knew I had to follow, there was no way to extrapolate.

And so, instead of searching for my lost self, for my freedom, as I could have when I lost Thomas, I searched for the thick relief that would come from plugging my gaping hole with a reliable stop from among the only world I knew. I looked for something that would save my life, for a relationship that would last forever. Because, after all—what was it for a person to gain the whole world, yet forfeit her own soul?

The engagement was my suggestion. My husband-to-be, a very accommodating person, asked me to marry him with a diamond ring that had a flaw in it, because it was cheaper that way, and we didn't want to complicate our lives with debts. Anyway, you couldn't see the defect unless you knew what you were looking for. I felt happy and relieved to finally join the ranks of my Witness friends who had all married at ages eighteen, nineteen, and twenty; I had achieved a moral way of life, which was the most important thing. We were to be married in October. I spent many days of my engagement wondering who would break the news to Thomas about my marriage: His mom? A friend? Would he have a sinking feeling in his stomach? Would his mouth become dry with regret?

Meanwhile, my husband was an uncomplicated person and well liked by the congregation. He would lay his head on my shoulder at friends' houses or in movies, and though I liked him, too, I was so corrupted within that I would cringe inside. He seemed to me to be childlike. He had a passivity that made him very easy to get along with, yet to me it seemed like an indifference to the world and to life. But indifference to life was a good quality for someone who was in a holding pattern waiting for Armageddon, and by being with him, I would be able to focus on the important things. He was the opposite of Thomas and the relationship was lifeless, and really that was perfect, given the times we were living in. The last days of this evil system were a time to focus on one thing: preaching. And my husband would never leave me, also unlike Thomas. In my naivety, I didn't realize that meant I would have to be the one to leave, an act that had no small consequences in our religion.

We planned the wedding over that summer. Full of sincerity, my grandmother sewed me a beautiful white dress that belied my less than virginal state, though she probably knew the truth, given that I had once been disfellowshipped. It was a copy of one I had tried on in a fancy wedding store, which my sister had surreptitiously taken pictures of from just above her purse so that we could re-create the design, given that I could not afford to buy it. I wore long white gloves and a veil my sister made from the fabric of the veil she had worn at her own wedding, which had taken place five years previous, the day after she turned nineteen.

I felt out of place at my wedding. Just over a year before, I had been shunned, treated as though I did not exist by the people from my congregation who were now invited here to share this day with me. They barely knew me. I walked between the brothers and sisters, who were having fun, eating, and laughing. Not knowing who to talk to, I felt like I was still on the outside, with my false dress and eyes that already wandered to bus windows, looking for my old love.

I take responsibility for the unhappiness of the relationship. The spouse-to-be who goes through with a marriage while thinking they might be in love with someone else on a wedding day is, in my belief, at fault. How can it be any other way? I could blame our age, my unchristian unsubmissiveness, his withdrawal, our dysfunctional families. But the marriage doesn't have a fighting chance when you long for something else. Nearly nine years of marriage and of unhappiness were my fault.

On our wedding night, I unbuttoned my dress for my husband. As he fumbled with the last few clasps, I felt no excitement. He felt my indifference—I tried to act, but I am a terrible actor. I felt so bad for him, I hadn't meant to do this, I was just doing what everyone else did, this was what we did, what we were told to do, this was living the best life: courtship, marriage, chastity—we had done everything by the book. When we did things Jehovah's way we were always happier. I couldn't understand why it didn't feel right.

"I was in New York when I heard news of your wedding," Thomas reported to me in a blasé fashion when I bumped into him one afternoon in his neighborhood, six months after my wedding, where I had ended up on an invented errand. With a shit-eating grin on his face and crumbs from his sandwich at the corner of his mouth, I knew at this moment he fancied himself a Henry James character or a tortured artist; I had heard him discuss this on many occasions.

"I was visiting Martin—you know, the one I told you about who was previously disfellowshipped for being gay—in New York City, and we were in a café near Washington Square. . . ."

He trailed off. I was still not sure how or why the news had traveled to New York City, but then Thomas was not the type of person who would hear from the receiver of a beige phone mounted to the wall of his kitchen that his first love's marriage had been sealed. I knew him well enough to know he would tragically hear about my nuptials in some exotic locale. I was irritated at his stupid affectations and what he imagined himself to be. But yet I was here for very valid reasons on an invented errand to his street. I decided to return to hating him. I smiled and left, retreating across the bridge back to my neighborhood, my body trembling.

A few years into our marriage, one Saturday summer night I was playing Van Morrison with the windows open, the way Thomas or I would have in the old days, relishing the beauty of the lyrics, or the music, or the night. My husband came home and I tried to find a way through what was wrong between us, to open myself again, to find some way to be together. I put on the song I had awaited his return to share, to start a conversation that to me would equal intimacy, connection. He sat on the sofa and stared at me while nodding his head in distant interest, hands on knees. It wasn't like we didn't get along, it was more that our minds never seemed to match. I fell silent, and he, after a while, fell asleep.

I went outside of our apartment and closed the door quietly behind me, into the darkness, down to the rocks on the water behind the planetarium at the beach, where no one was around. I lay down, and the rocks jabbed into my shoulder blades and the kelp slimed on my arms. I breathed in the air and experienced alone the things I wished we could have together. Everything around me moved as part of a whole and entered me, no different from my own pulse. It felt sacred. But then the cold of the rocks started to hurt and the kelp crept up the side of my arm and I began to understand that I had no control and that no one can make someone fit the size of the hole and the seal was never sound and my hermetic dreams of safety were slowly leaking. And on that day, after three or four years of trying, I could not feel anything for this man who was my husband. My life with him did not feel like my own, and I was here on the rocks by myself, enjoying them jut into my back because at least they responded, even if it hurt. I want more, I thought. I have known more.

And I had worked hard, I had done all I could to stay busy, so that the time until the real life would pass more quickly. I had preached on in hopes that a will strong enough could bring Armageddon, the fire that would destroy this marriage and this life and rebirth it in paradise on Earth, where pandas would cuddle my husband and me, filling the dark places inside us with rainbows and light. Where I would love him and no longer crave anything more.

But despite all these efforts, by the time I was lying on these rocks, I had begun constantly to think about the life I'd had in the neighborhood across the water from here and of my old lover. I prayed to God to stop my thoughts, but he did not help me. I was obsessed. I was the stalker, but I began to feel watched, because what I was feeling was so immoral and wrong. I knew Jehovah could see me, even though he was not one to listen.

Yet my city is a small city, and it was easy to pretend to oneself that one was not doing the thing that one was doing. I looked for Thomas on the streets we had fought on, kissed on. His apartment—or as close as I dared to get to it—was always my destination, even if I never made it there. I imagined he was home. That he looked for me outside. If not now, surely yesterday or last month or at some point of some day. I stared inside every bus window as the driver flashed past, wondering if it was his route now, seeking his lithe silhouette, which sat ever so slightly toward the front edge of the seat, and for his puffy brown curls in the blue short-sleeved Transit Authority–issue button-down. I looked for him with the agony of the mother of a kidnapped child, who has lost not only what she loves most, but also a part of herself.

That world I had lived in across this bridge still existed for me, as if I had been a man who had walked on the moon, looking back at its bright circle from the ground. It was not a parallel universe; it was a forgotten planet. A paradise without God. Our new world was there. Reading books all day and all night while trying not to think about being killed by God, hoping there was a little more time to live, feeling more religious than we ever had at seeing blood-red skies or smelling the sea when he drove me past the bay to work. His bed island in the room where we had unexpected and confused sex, for the first time, both of us laughing afterward at our discovery of it. He under the covers with a flashlight, us both figuring out my parts, his parts being so obvious and all, and I trying to make sense of myself and the body that I didn't even know yet, through him. We tasted of coffee in the pot, smelled of soft slept-on black cotton sheets flecked with dried skin. We sounded like bare skin sticking to the leather of the sofa on which we would make love as we learned how to do it better and better, and fights so loud that the neighbor would comment to Thomas about them in the elevator, or so he said.

The only way to remain in this paradise was to forget everything from our former life—a no-man's-land between us and it. And once paradise was lost, the only way to live was by making the distance between myself and it so big, it retreated into nothingness.

And now, I was across the world. I had dragged this husband, the one whom I had done everything with in God's way, to the farthest place I could imagine, far enough away to escape what haunted me, to throw myself into the work I had to do in order to not die. I had found a place where I no longer had to look in bus windows or go for walks with only one terminus. I had filled up my head with words in another language so there was no room to think anymore. I had cut myself off from all means of contact in a country where even an e-mail sent was read by someone. This was the only place for me. I would wait for paradise here.

The taxi driver slowed and asked my husband in Chinese if this was the place. There was only a gate, with a long driveway, but an archway above the entrance said in Chinese RAINBOW HOTEL. It seemed right, so we paid the fare and walked through the gate to the main door.

In the lobby, there was a small waterfall and pool lit by blue and pink lights, and just past it, the elevator. We didn't want to draw any attention to ourselves so we entered it quickly and proceeded to the floor on which the meeting was to be held. There we found the door number we were looking for and knocked.

A brother with a European accent opened the door and welcomed us with a smile and a handshake. Behind him were about thirty people, some standing around chatting, others sitting, waiting for the meeting to begin. At the front of the room, a podium sat in expectation, and rows of chairs had been lined up just as they would have been in any Kingdom Hall on the planet.

Somehow, in this three-star hotel in China, behind a locked door, we had reentered our world.

A few weeks had passed since our arrival in Shanghai. We needed to figure out a way to earn a living. Jehovah's Witnesses, the vast majority of them anyway, have to support themselves while spending much of their time in the preaching work. We had purchased a three-month "business visa" through an agent in Hong Kong and planned to stay indefinitely, but we didn't have much savings left to live on.

After a week of looking, my husband found a part-time job in an English kindergarten, teaching, just as many foreigners do when they come to China. Neither of us had gone to university, and therefore normally would never have qualified for a teaching position, nor been able to get a legitimate work visa for that matter. But a few years before, at a time when fake degrees were showing up for $99 on the Internet, a scam more holy in nature popped up in the Jehovah's Witness community. This involved a university in an American town I had never heard of making its online degrees a notch less fake by crediting the preaching hours Jehovah's Witnesses had done as work experience that could be put toward offsetting the four years' worth of time required in class to achieve a bachelor's degree. In reality, there was no time in class, but instead you wrote a "thesis" essay and took a three-hundred-question, multiple-choice, open-book exam, and were then awarded your piece of paper.

The *Watchtower* magazines that we handed out to the public touted us as the most honest, upright people in the world. That being said, most of us who were trying to sell ourselves as English teachers in order to support ourselves in our preaching work had been admonished not to pursue education beyond a basic high school diploma. This created a difficulty, because the Governing Body was encouraging people to go to foreign lands to preach, and to do that we needed jobs. Most jobs for foreigners in other countries involved teaching or having some other specialized skill.

For obvious reasons, earning a degree at an actual university that would have taught critical thinking skills and emphasized training for a successful career was not permissible. And sure enough, almost any Witness I knew who had rebelled against this edict was eventually disfellowshipped for something or another. But this $3,000 scam degree was no problem at all. In fact, it was encouraged by some of those in higher-up positions, who reminded us of a Bible principle I have since seen the Governing Body use to lie in child abuse court cases: theocratic warfare. Meaning, if being dishonest will do something to advance Jehovah's will, then it's okay to make an exception and keep one's clean conscience.

Therefore, many of us pioneer missionaries jumped at the chance to get a fake degree. We avoided the dangers of higher education by paying $3,000 to write whatever double-spaced essay we were capable of, and fill out some multiple-choice circles in pencil.

But then there was the problem of money. Three thousand dollars was a fortune to us. Six thousand dollars for both of us was totally out of the question. So we decided that we would borrow enough money for one degree from my grandmother, who as a nearly lifelong Witness really had only about that much saved to her name. My husband would apply and write the essay, while I would do all the questions and help with research for his paper. I sat in a room for three weeks of one summer we were home, tapping away, making edits to his essay on my keyboard, and filling in multiple-choice circles so that my husband could get his "degree." But it worked. He got the certificate with the beautiful scrolling font and the town name no one had heard of, the job in the school, and a more legitimate work visa than the one we had purchased from god-knows-who in Hong Kong. As his spouse, I was allowed a residency permit. Like my religion, China was a society that made compromises to get what it wanted, and no one ever checked or found out that this university didn't even exist, or that this man was clearly not qualified to be teaching in an educational institution.

As for me, I didn't have many job skills, purposely. Like most Jehovah's Witnesses, I hadn't done much more than preach my whole adult life while supporting myself with part-time jobs. So, to start out, I did what many foreigners of dubious backgrounds who came to China did—I put an ad on the Internet advertising myself as a private English tutor.

My first student was a young Shanghainese woman who worked in a large American company. When I first heard her speak Chinese to someone on a phone call she made during our class, I noticed that she had a thick northern accent. This surprised me, because she was short, like many southern Chinese people, with the rounded, large features of a Shanghainese, yet she had the voice of a tall, angular Xinjiang-ren, or resident of Xinjiang. I later found out that she had in fact been raised in Xinjiang, the Chinese territory that was more like one of the "-stans" than a part of China, a region where the people looked more Middle Eastern than Han in origin. Her parents had been relocated there from Shanghai during the Cultural Revolution for the crime of being doctors. They were sent to work on farms to be reeducated and stayed there even after the Cultural Revolution ended, having had a daughter and become accustomed to the life, and fearing what their reception in Shanghai would be like if they returned.

Their daughter, my student, had moved back to Shanghai herself after graduating from university, being allotted a special permit to move to the city, though she had not been born here and so didn't have the coveted native residency permit that gave a person by birthright the ability to work and live in one of the first-tier cities. She now worked at General Electric, and her parents were soon going to move back in with her in Shanghai, as she needed to support them.

Another woman contacted me, wanting a conversation class together with her husband. When the couple arrived in my living room, the husband introduced himself by his English name, "Money." They told me they had a young son, and making conversation, I asked what his name was. "Cash," the man said. This "choosing your own name" seemed to be a two-way street—my Chinese name, Zi An, which I used as my under-cover name, sounded like a mysterious Chinese spy novel char-acter to my ears but sounded quite odd to the Chinese, I had been told.

As I set out teaching my students, all of whom were highly educated, I hoped they wouldn't ask me where I went to uni-versity, seeing as I didn't even have a fake university name to drop. But to my relief, I discovered that most of the Chinese people I encountered, at least those who were around my age or younger, knew almost everything they needed to know about English already—they just couldn't speak it well. All they really needed was practice conversing with someone they felt comfortable with. I was happy to not have to worry about cur-riculum or explaining English grammar, something I wasn't too clear on myself, and to instead sit with them and talk for two hours and be paid at the conclusion of it.

It was the easiest living I had ever made, and while I did see improvement in my students' English over time, I also learned a lot about where I was living from them. In my home country, the atrocities I knew of from history books had not occurred during the generation I was part of, or my parents' generation, for that matter. But in Shanghai, these histories were fresh; they had taken place only a few decades earlier. The witnesses and participants to them were all around me. Some of the neighbors, teachers, local shop owners, and others whom I interacted with were people who must have lived through the Cultural Revolution. Some had marched with Mao, had undergone famine, or had been part of the Red Guard burning the books at universities and pulling up the flowers from the bourgeois flower beds.

It wasn't something anyone talked about—no one was advertising the role they had played, or who had been the victims. It was not a subject that was broached in polite company, and a cultural amnesia seemed to be the practical means of dealing with what had happened on these streets and in these buildings. But still, the past permeated the air of the city, and the more I understood about what people had been through, it struck me how the violent, distant history of my own country was only an abstraction for me. Here, the history was so recent it had been interwoven into their lives—it was what I saw in the weight of their expressions, what I felt in the tension on the street that simmered, ready to explode, and in the glare of the windows of the Peace Hotel, once breached by bodies thrown out of them.

And it was here in my student named Money. A legacy in the hidden depths of a population that was not only living in a Communist society but also at the same time climbing the corporate ladder and naming their children after currency.

It all seemed so contradictory. Both they and I had these lives that were created out of circumstance, accidents of birth, and we went along in them, carried forward by the decisions made for us long before we were alive, our participation in the whole scheme making us feel ownership—that indeed this was our life, our possession, our creation. But what things lay dormant? Lodged in our gray matter were there other parts of ourselves—lives we did not have the opportunity to carry out or the circumstances required to invent or the courage to do something about? What other life were we capable of? There seemed to be two sides to Money, the side formed by what he was born into, and the side that seeped out, in the form of currency, in this living room.

And then there was me, sitting across from them, with my fake name and life built inside my organization. I was an uneducated preacher posing as an English teacher, my presence here not what I claimed it was. I was out to change the course of other people's lives, and their children's lives, and their children's children's lives. I somehow had the effrontery to try to alter the course of their history, to urge these people to make over their lives into the shape of mine, when I had never even considered how my own life had come to look as it did.

n 1909 in Brooklyn, the borough of a thousand churches, a wealthy man from Pennsylvania bought a brick building on a steep street just south of the Brooklyn Bridge, across the river from Manhattan. Blocks away from where Walt Whitman had set to type the first editions of *Leaves of Grass*, a small, relatively unknown group that called themselves the "Bible Students" was regrouping, with this building as their hub.

Their leader, Charles Taze Russell, was feeling discouraged after another failed prediction that the world would end. But he was not deterred. With this new building, printing presses, and followers growing across the Eastern Seaboard, Russell was confident that God had shown himself to be with them, and he pushed on with renewed zeal and revised dates. Spending his days overlooking the same East River that had inspired Whitman to write verse, he rewrote his own inspired prose that warned of the world's imminent, violent end and urged all to join him so that they, too, could live forever in paradise on Earth.

Russell had always been interested in religion and as a

young man had painted fire and brimstone Bible verses on fences around his hometown as a pastime. As he got older, he studied various religions to try and find the answers to the many questions of life that plagued him, but he never found anything that satisfied him. As he neared disillusionment, he met a man named William Miller, who had founded a religious movement, Millerism, which was the precursor to the Seventh-day Adventist Church. Russell found his own interest in apocalypse mirrored in Miller, who had used the prophecies in the book of Daniel to calculate the return of Christ. He joined the Millerites for a time, but after a series of distressing miscalculations and disappointments over being stood up by Jesus, Russell broke off and decided the only answer was to form his own sect. He used his father's money to travel to the Pyramids at Giza to seek answers to the riddle of the last days, and he focused his mind and energies on interpreting the timeline for the end of the world.

Like Miller before him, Russell didn't live to see his predictions come true. Shortly after his volumes *Studies in the Scriptures* had been dispatched from the printery on Columbia Heights, he died. But his apocalypse was not extinguished with him. It, along with his money, was passed on to a series of successors, who, like him, were surprised at the close of each day to see the skyline of Manhattan still intact across the river. For the next hundred years, Armageddon did not come.

Like a home that fills up with comfortable clutter as the years pass, this group, which had been founded under Russell's conviction that no organized religious structure was needed to find truth, flourished in limbo. It accumulated writings, doctrines, rules—and followers, millions of them. A hierarchy seemed to build itself without anyone noticing, and it became a bureaucracy that rivaled any large human institution.

A Governing Body anointed itself through God's "holy spirit," and eventually the eight male leaders who made up that group would, from their carpeted offices overlooking Manhattan, come to preside over almost every aspect of their followers' spiritual, moral, and material lives. Children were born into this organization and grew up in it; the estates of people who were never supposed to grow old and die were left to it. Steady donations funded the accumulation of over 3.2 million square feet of property in Brooklyn Heights, much of it connected by a network of underground tunnels. From these buildings and printeries, the Governing Body, now referring to itself as the "Faithful and Discreet Slave," oversaw what became one of the biggest publishing entities in the world, and it rallied its members to carry the message of impending destruction to the corners of the Earth by way of an aggressive proselytizing campaign. Those who did not listen were simply scratched off until the next month these preachers came around, when they had another chance to get on the right side of God's genocide.

And like this, they kept knocking. And waiting, with each passing day taking them one day closer to "the real life." As the years passed, and the portions of their lives in this old world dragged on as predictions of the world's end in 1878, 1881, 1914, 1918, 1925, 1930, 1975, and more failed to materialize, the leaders edited the old editions of their publications to soften some of those proclamations. The believers took comfort in the words of Jesus that "regarding that day or that hour, only the Father in heaven knows," and forgave the miscalculations of their leaders, knowing that the scriptures say the light gets brighter as the day draws near. Jehovah would progressively reveal the truth to his people at the time of the end.

Many of the religions that came out of the Second Great Awakening in the northeastern United States, including the Millerites, had formed as a reaction to the growing secularism of society. These religions appeared quickly and with fervor, but in time, many of them fizzled out, as did a number of sects that had splintered off from them. However, those that had charismatic leaders, or had sufficiently reinvented themselves and propagated their ranks through intensive preaching efforts, survived in new forms, and remnants of their teachings influenced some of the Apocalyptic movements that have arisen in more recent decades (for example, the Branch Davidians, in Waco, Texas, who, tired of waiting for Armageddon, found themselves in an apocalypse not of God's provenance).

As for Russell, there were many other people who wanted to be in paradise, too. His humble group of Bible students thrived. By 1975, when another one of the dates circled along the bumpy timeline to the purported end of the world had come and gone, Russell's small group of followers had morphed into a highly structured organization with followers so devoted they were willing to refuse blood transfusions even if it cost the lives of their own children, because they believed God forbade putting blood into their bodies, and to shun anyone, including members of their own family, who disagreed with the organization's official teachings. To approximately eight million people on Earth today, this organization is the one true religion,

God's kingdom on Earth, and the only source of truth. And thanks to a genius rebranding effort in the 1930s by an ill-tempered, six-foot-eight-inch man named Joseph Rutherford, who in the 1930s proclaimed "Millions Now Living Will Never Die!," this organization today has the name "Jehovah's Witnesses."

My grandparents on both my mother's and father's sides became Jehovah's Witnesses when they were adults. My mother's mother, Kay, already had two young children when an aunt of her husband, Jack, converted to the faith after a proselytizer came to her door in their prairie city. The aunt thereafter "witnessed" to Jack for years, attempting to convert him, to the point where he secretly became convinced that he had found the truth.

Yet my grandfather did not bring up the topic of religion until years later, when my grandmother—a very intuitive, independent, wise woman—had reason to suspect he was having an affair. When confronted about the purported dalliance, he knew full well that if he admitted it, my grandmother would leave him. So he denied the affair—to his deathbed—but to save his marriage, he said that the time had come for him and Kay to take the offer his aunt had made to study the Bible with them. Jack was no dummy himself, and though he had become convinced that the things his aunt was saying were truths, he also knew that the Jehovah's Witnesses forbade divorce. The last thing he wanted was to lose his smart, sharp wife.

My grandmother, a schoolteacher, was not a submissive woman before she became a Jehovah's Witness. Afterward, of course, she had no choice, but she finally agreed to my grandfather's suggestion of a Bible study only under the condition that she was doing it to prove wrong these men who came to their house once a week to study the Bible.

For the next year, she spent two hours or so a week arguing with the men who sat in their living room, teaching her and her husband, who was largely silent. With great patience, they answered her questions and countered her arguments, using their books that had the answers to every question, and their kindness, which was unflappable, to win her over. And win her over they eventually did—as soon as my grandmother became convinced she had the truth, she became just as forcefully for it as she had been against it. My grandfather followed her into the religion, and they were baptized when my mother was about twelve years old. The old Christmas decorations were abruptly dumped on the street for the garbageman, birthday parties were now forbidden as "pagan," worldly family members were witnessed to, and if they rejected the truth, kept at arm's length.

Now, instead of fighting, three times a week my grandmother put on her jewelry and heels, my grandfather donned the one tie he had purchased for the purpose, and the family piled into their boat of a car to drive through the frozen Alberta streets to the Kingdom Hall, where the brothers left their vehicles running in the parking lots so that their engine blocks would not turn to ice and refuse to start when it was time to return home again.

My mother, an extrovert, later told me that she never really believed all that they were saying at the meetings, at least not entirely, but that she enjoyed the social aspect of the congregation, the friends that she made there. My grandmother had always been harsh to her and critical, rejecting her for her brother, and she felt accepted by the warm embrace of the community. That brother, his mother's favorite, on the other hand, never really took to things and left for the "world" when he was sixteen, moving out and becoming a drug dealer. That was what happened when you left, we were told, pointing to our uncle as a cautionary tale. People who left the truth became drug dealers and they went to jail—as he did, many years later.

Those who stayed in the truth, however, were rewarded— with warm friends, the guidance of Jehovah's holy spirit, answers to all of life's unsettling questions, and love—as long as they stayed in the faith.

It was that simple. It was black, and it was white. The organization was good and the world was bad, and this was something that was easy for human beings to understand, which was much of its appeal. The truth should be simple, we always said.

It was rare to meet a Witness who was not wholly committed, because this was not the kind of religion in which one could be a Sunday Christian. Paradise was as real to us as a memory—and even though it wasn't something concrete, our minds were already there in it. We had allocated everyday existence its place but were in reality just waiting to live. And unlike the events in our memories, which no amount of pining could bring us back to, if we harnessed our individual nature and did what was right, we would keep the approval of our peers and our families and our community—but most of all, our God—and live forever in this coming paradise without any death, sorrow, sickness, or suffering.

Of course, like in many things, for the greatest chance at success, it is best to start training when you are young. My father had also been raised a Witness and married my mother, who was a Witness, because marrying outside the faith would result in being "marked" as bad association. The basic path for any Jehovah's Witness is to marry young, and quickly, before the temptation to have premarital sex causes you to sin, and then, when and if children come along, to start their education in the truth young, to provide a buffer that will shore them up against the "world" that they would inevitably encounter when they started school (if Armageddon hadn't come by then). This life prescription was laid out before us constantly—at meetings, at conventions, and by our parents.

But sometime after my older sister was born, my parents stopped going to the meetings. By the time I was born, two and a half years later, they had settled into a religious rut during which they attended just one meeting a year—the most important one, of course, the memorial of Jesus' death—for fear that not to attend that one would seal all of our fates when Armageddon arrived. It wasn't that they didn't believe—they taught me that I was a Jehovah's Witness, even though we rarely set foot in a Kingdom Hall or spoke to another Witness.

Though I was never told why, I can imagine reasons they

stopped going regularly. For one thing, the Witness way of life is exhausting, and dragging two or three children to meetings in the evenings after bedtime or on the weekends is not a light demand. The weekends were for service, and if you didn't go out preaching regularly, the elders would come and visit you to find out why. My father was also a very shy man, and I think he was most comfortable in his house, surrounded by his kids, his TV, and his wine. Socializing did not come naturally to him, and my mother wasn't about to bundle us all up in the thirty-degrees-below-zero weather for the sake of her social life. She was outgoing and found neighbor friends for that.

Growing up in this environment gave my brother and sister and me the worst of both worlds, in a way. We didn't have the community we would have had if we had been Witnesses who attended meetings and service. But we also couldn't go to birthday parties, and didn't get Christmas presents. We had to leave the school gym during Christmas carol singalongs, and on hot dog day my mom had to bring special hot dogs to the school that were set aside to boil for us, since the regular hot dogs might have blood by-products in them, and blood in any form could not be put into the body. It was mortifying. But in the unquestioning way of children, we knew that we were not like the other kids. They were going to die at Armageddon, and we, the special hot dog eaters, would live. This, for us, was a reality we did not question.

This was all we knew of life, and for a long time I thought that was how it was for all Witnesses. That was until second grade, when for Halloween, we were given an art project where we had to use orange and black construction paper to make a silhouette for the wall in some kind of Halloween theme. As a Witness, I did not celebrate this pagan holiday. But as an astute observer of the line between the religion that was a mystery even to me and gaining acceptance from my school peers, I chose to cut out an ambiguous owl on a branch in front of a full moon as my subject. In orange and black, next to the jack-o'-lanterns and ghosts, it wouldn't telegraph "Bully her!" But if my parents happened to come in the room on parents' night, no one could really say it was *definitely* a Halloween object.

Then came the day the teacher stapled all of the artwork to the corkboard, and as I scanned the orange and black paneling the wall, proud that mine was the only owl among a sea of jack-o'-lanterns and other Satan-objects, my eye stopped on a strange rectangular black blob against an orange sky. On the blob, written in yellow chalk, were smeared the words "Kingdom Hall of Jehovah's Witnesses." What? I saw the name "Leesa" written at the bottom. It was the new girl. So she was a Witness, too. A real Witness, apparently, unlike me. It was strange to have an authentic one in the class, setting the bar suddenly, and I knew now that my owl, despite being one of God's creations, showed me up for the imposter Witness I was. It *did* look a little spooky. When the teacher returned our artworks to us on November 1, I threw mine in the garbage.

Years later, when Leesa was sixteen, she got pregnant by a worldly boy and had to drop out of school. Situations like these sometimes seemed to occur more frequently for Witnesses, who had lived such sheltered, controlled existences compared with the population at large. A teenage Witness boy or girl is not taught about birth control, because it is taken as a given that they will not be having sex. When things went wrong, they seemed to go terribly wrong.

Though my parents had managed to make their children think that they were Jehovah's Witnesses, most likely to salve their own consciences, my grandmother Kay was a sharp woman, and she knew that we were shortly going to be eaten up by the world if someone didn't do something to intervene. When it came to her attention that my parents, who lived on the other side of the city from her congregation, were no longer attending the meetings, she was very concerned. She couldn't get anywhere with convincing my parents to go back, nor could she extract from my parents the reason why they had stopped going to the meetings. But I do remember once, much later, my grandma confiding in me how grateful she was that my parents had given her unlimited access to us spiritually. They were probably happy to have someone do the work that God expected of them and let us go with her out of ambivalence.

I didn't really know the difference, but when my grandmother started taking us kids with her to the meetings, I began to understand what the consequences of us not going to the meetings would be. I was about eight years old when it started to become clear.

When we were dropped off at Grandma's for the weekend, she would serve us pierogis on black plates with white cream sauce flecked with dill from her front flower bed, borscht she'd made that morning, and sauerkraut from the jar bubbling in the corner of her kitchen. I knew she loved us, and though she was often stern, a glint in her eye would tell us when she was in a fun mood. In many ways, she mothered me more than my own mother—who had often confessed that she felt she would have made a better aunt than mom. I remember once my grandmother overseeing my bath in her schoolteacher way, and when I tried to get out, she asked me if I had washed my "pee-pee." I had no idea what she was talking about; my mom had never told me to do any such thing, as she would also not in the future teach me about periods, or about sex.

After we all had lunch, I would go up the nubby gold carpeted stairs, past the walls made from white-painted cheap concrete bricks, to the bookshelves in the second room of her government-subsidized row house and find a *Reader's Digest* anthology to read while lying on the guest cot. Or we'd sit out on the concrete front stoop and chat or shell peas from her garden in the flower bed while looking across the table-flat field to the Southgate Mall parking lot. She didn't let us watch TV. Anyway, the sofas were too hard to sit on for long.

On many afternoons, from downstairs came the warm clack of Scrabble tiles, their corners rounded from years of games. Friends from her congregation would come over to play a game on my grandma's super-deluxe edition with the lazy Susan base. My grandma's schoolteacher past had given her renown among the other Witnesses as the Scrabble Queen, and she was usually the only one who could put all her letters down in one turn. I would tiptoe into her bedroom, looking for something to try on in front of the full-length mirror—my usual strings of pearls or clip-on earrings, some too-big high heels.

My grandmother, like most Witnesses, never had much money, but she always could dress to the nines. She had a stalker once, when she was seventy-five. My grandfather had died years earlier, and she would come home from her meetings or preaching dressed up to find a letter in the mailbox. It was from a secret admirer who wanted to meet her at Woodward's department store for a coffee. Once, years later, Grandma confessed to me that she met him on one occasion. This was shocking, Armageddon-doom-worthy behavior—something a teenager would have done behind her parents' back—a date at a cafeteria with a worldly man. They met on the top floor, with windows overlooking the parking lot. My grandma was tempted, she told me, out of flattery. He was sixty-five. She said she now understood how hard it was for all the young people "in the truth."

The first time I remember going to the meeting with my grandma was one of these weekends. My sister and I woke early on Sunday morning and put on the matching ruffled corduroy dresses and white blouses my mom—who made up for what she lacked in mothering skills with creative ones—had sewn for us for the first day of school earlier in the year. Mine was blue, my sister's pink. My sister yanked open the long, winglike door of my grandma's Ford Thunderbird, and we climbed into the cavernous, dark red backseat. Grandma drove to the Kingdom Hall while our little bodies, not wearing seat belts in that era, went sliding across the smooth leather seats whenever she turned a corner.

When we walked into the Kingdom Hall, it smelled like books and perfume, laced with a twist of lemon cleaner. The carpets were vacuumed and we made new tracks as we followed Grandma to the coatroom to take off our winter coats and scarves. We walked into the main auditorium, and my grandma put some Bibles and *Watchtowers* down on the seats to reserve them for the three of us (my brother, who was a few years younger, had been left at home with my parents). I felt shy in the growing crowd of strangers, bubbles of them forming here and there around the hall. My world was small, between home and school, but I still remember the warm feeling I had when we were greeted at the Kingdom Hall. My grandmother's friends doted on us and welcomed me like I had never felt welcomed anywhere in this world. Here I found what I could not get at home.

When it was time for the meeting to start, a brother cleared his throat into the microphone at the podium onstage and a piercing ring of feedback alerted everyone to take their seats. We all stood up, and the PA system piped in the notes for song number 171, "A Victory Song." We sang a few verses about God killing everyone who wasn't one of his people on Judgment Day:

See now all nations opposing the Sov'reign, Jehovah.
Though mightier than Pharaoh, they too will suffer shame.
Doom now awaits them; they will not survive Armageddon.
Soon ev'ryone will know that Jehovah is God's name.

The march tempo made it sound a little festive, rousing even. When the song was over, another man came up to the microphone to give a prayer, just like Dad did for dinnertime, but longer, and I closed my eyes while still standing when I saw everyone else do that. We said "amen" when he finished, and the meeting began.

The brother introduced another man, who went up to the podium with notes and a Bible. There was a Bible passage written on a panel on the wall to his left, painted in a brown italicized font. *"They will not prevail against you, for 'I [Jehovah] am with you . . . to deliver you.'*—Jer. 1:19," it read. The paper had bubbled where it had been glued to the wood paneling of the frame. The speaker wore a suit, brown as well. He began to talk for what would be forty-five minutes on the topic "How We Know We Are Living in the Last Days."

It was hard to sit still. And in spite of the constrictions of my corduroy dress, I was dying to lie down on the carpet and feign sleep like I glimpsed a little boy doing in the row in front of us. I knew my grandma wouldn't have it, and when I squirmed she handed me a pen and paper and told me to write down the scriptures the elder called out for everyone to turn to in their Bibles and read along with him. Obediently, I tried to catch what he was saying, writing out "songs" for "psalms," my pen trailing off halfway through the twelve attempts at "Deuteronomy."

Standing again for the rousing song at intermission helped—something about God's arrangement of marriage, and how joyous it was for women to have men as their head. After the song I was less sleepy, but I needed something to occupy me for the ensuing hour, as a new brother had settled onto the stage, crinkly *Watchtower* magazine in hand. This man in his too-small suit propped himself against the podium as he waited for a paragraph from the magazine to be read by his assistant. When the reading was finished, people put up their hands to answer the question printed at the bottom of the page. Then the man chose someone from the audience to give a comment or answer. When he called out a name, "Brother so-and-so," that person would state their answer into a roving microphone, which was carried around by a young pimpled brother. At times, if no hands were raised, the man at the front would lift a hankie to his forehead, wipe away the sweat, and after an awkward silence, exhort everyone that the *Watchtower* study was meant for commenting, and this was a form of worship to Jehovah, so please raise your hands.

Luckily, a plump lady in the row in front of me with black dyed hair, which may have been a wig, took pity on me. She was holding a yellow highlighter and looked back at me while wagging it at something she had underlined in her copy of the magazine. Shy as I felt, the mortification of raising my hand was mitigated by the excitement of killing time. That was not to mention how much I wanted to try talking into that microphone hockey-taped to a smooth wooden pole the brother would hold to your mouth if you were so chosen. The interminable meeting had taken on new life—the sheer terror of this new element was somehow attractive.

Next paragraph, the wigged sister turned around and, in a whisper, shouted to me encouragingly, "Jehovah!," pointing at her magazine paragraph again. I got a rush of anxiety and pride as I raised my hand, but I was too late—another little kid was called on. "Keep trying!" her face said. Finally, four paragraphs more and the raven hair craned back to me: "Jesus Christ!" The brother didn't know my name so he said, "The little sister with Sister Hawrelak." My hand was up and the pimpled teenager had strained his gangly arm out to reach my mouth with the mic and before I knew it I leaned forward and said, "Jesus Christ?" Someone clapped, Grandma nodded. It was probably the most attention I'd had in weeks. A warm happiness came over me.

Driving home in my grandma's Thunderbird, we stopped at the Southgate Mall. Grandma took me into Woodward's to buy a pair of shiny black rain boots.

Walking in the door to the aromas of my family home later that afternoon, I was quiet, as usual. It always hit me a little, the smell of the house; the intangible things seemed to have taken on importance in correlation to the degree to which the family itself seemed to lose its shape with each passing year.

My mom's cooking rotation, the shaggy carpet, the white Formica dresser filled with seersucker and hand-me-down T-shirts, the yellowing phone on the desk. They were stand-ins for the usual things of memories, for the warmth and closeness that did not reside here.

I walked past the living room. My dad, in his usual posture, was sprawled sideways on the tan carpet, watching TV with his polyester pant leg up on the increasingly threadbare stool, his daytime wine in his favorite goblet. He didn't really notice me, but he would have been happy to see me, he always was. I didn't like his shiny eyes when he drank, and so I avoided them—though of course I didn't think there was anything unusual about his drinking, since it was so routine. For a child, routine is everything.

I skirted past him and into my room and unpacked my overnight bag and smoothed out the *Watchtower* I had been given to take home, adding it to the collection of library books on the small night table between my sister's bed and mine.

Some days, when we were playing outside, my brother and sister and I came home to find the doors locked, our parents not answering our incessant ringing of the doorbell. When they finally called us in, we never asked them why they hadn't answered. What happened in our house was normal, to us; parents were people who rarely conversed with each other, and our own problems were things we took with us to bed, matters to push away in any way you could in order to find sleep after the sunlight of a long northern summer night had faded outside your bedroom blind.

One night, when I had a particularly long-lasting case of insomnia accompanied by my usual terrors of the Armageddon I heard so much about at the Kingdom Hall, I went out to my dad in front of the TV and asked him if he might be able to spank me, since crying myself to sleep had generally worked well in the past. This was the only kind of help I knew to seek from my parents.

Because my parents were preoccupied with other things, my main teacher had become books. My mother would take me along with her to the library, where she would sign out a shopping bag full of romance novels that she would hide under the couch so my dad wouldn't see she was reading them.

Wandering around waiting for her to yell my name, bored and watchful, I found the young adult shelves. My parents had taught me very little about life, about the world, about anything. Maybe it was because they believed the world was ending, so what was the point. At home, we had a few books, but the one that stood out most was *My Book of Bible Stories,* a children's book that had both pictures of children in a garden cuddling with a lion, and pictures of children dying at Armageddon, depending on which story you opened to. But here in the library there was the thrill of words that taught me about other people bit by bit. I would read three books at a time, putting one book down after finishing one chapter and moving on to the next book and another chapter.

My favorites were stories of kids who lived in New York City, who had a superintendent (some sort of troll, I presumed, who lived in the basement of apartment buildings) and who sat on fire escapes to dream and pass the time. The same New York I heard about on the radio around this time, in the dulcet tones of Christopher Cross, as I was transported around in the plush of the backseat of my dad's light blue Oldsmobile. I would look out the back window at the passing streetlights of our small prairie city, "Arthur's Theme" playing on the radio, dreaming of a life in New York City, where "the best that you can do is fall in love." I wondered how people got there, how it was that they got to be there, while I was here in this cold prairie tundra.

I received my first Jehovah's Witness book shortly after my initial meeting. It was a green hardcover New World Translation of the Bible with a spine that cracked when you opened it and onionskin pages that stuck together when it was new. In the back of the Bible, I found the only pictures in the book: maps of Paul's missionary tours, which I would flip through sometimes. There was another map on the front inside cover that had an X marked at the "possible site of the Garden of Eden," somewhere in Jordan. I wrote my name in my awkward, too-big script there, somewhere between the Sea of Galilee and the former paradise, a proud owner. I sometimes opened my Bible to read it, but since I could not really understand much of what I saw in there, I would return to my Beverly Cleary.

The summer I got that Bible, Grandma took us to the District Convention—an annual event at a giant sports arena. Witness volunteers first scrubbed the building with enough soap and water to remove all vestiges of dirt and worldliness, then ten thousand or so Witnesses would listen to three or four days' worth of talks and seminars developed to train them to be more loyal Jehovah's Witnesses, better preachers, to endure until Armageddon, to for God's sake never allow oneself to be dirtied by the world ("world" meaning college, a career, friends, sports, interests, hobbies, and anything or anyone else outside the dominion of the Jehovah's Witness planet).

New members were also publicly baptized at these conventions. People were encouraged to request to be baptized whenever they felt ready to make a dedication to the organization and to Jehovah. It could happen at any age, but those who had been born into the religion were constantly encouraged to do it from a young age, some as young as eight or nine years old. I got baptized when I was fourteen. On that day I was on the floor of the concourse, where a large inflatable pool had been erected. My bathing suit was modestly covered by a plain white T-shirt as a brother dunked me underwater for all in the stadium to see. I heard the applause underwater, and it burst out in a crescendo as I was lifted from the water. That part was thrilling, but for the most part, these days of talks felt interminable, and the monotony of the old male speakers went on uninterrupted for hours. Respite came only once in a while, when they raised their voice as their talk reached its climax about Armageddon or Jehovah, which would signal the audience to applaud.

There were, on the other hand, delicious hamburgers you could buy with ten meal tickets, which you purchased for ten cents each. Lunches with potato chips and chocolate or vanilla pudding for four meal tickets, the pudding always frozen, for some reason, perhaps to save on refrigeration. At lunch, the congregation kids would roam around the top of the arena in their dresses and suits. I longed to play with the children I saw, but they didn't know me. I was the imitation Jehovah's Witness who didn't know that Smurfs were Satanic things that jumped out of wallpaper in bedrooms (a common belief among Witnesses at the time), or that I shouldn't say "bless you" when someone sneezed, eat Lucky Charms cereal, or play Pac-Man on our Atari, because of the ghosts.

Between my boredom and as many bathroom breaks as I could get away with, I tried to be good and pay attention to what was said. I could sense it was important, and Grandma had trained me well enough at the meetings that I knew what a side glance from her meant. One technique for sitting still was to watch the digital LED clock flip the minutes away. Or gaze at the hockey banners as they flapped in the draft of the air-conditioning, which was always either too cold or not nearly cold enough, every year. I would watch the clean-shaven fathers and modestly dressed submissive mothers walking their restless children up and down the stairs to the concourse, zombie-like in their inner peace, finding myself wishing I was them and had a baby to look after so I could have an excuse to walk around.

Another more Grandmother-pleasing method of passing the time was to busily occupy myself flipping the pages of the green Bible every time the speaker would mention a scripture. Everyone else was doing it. "Acts 4:34!," the brother would say, the sound echoing back to me from across the arena, being slowly overwhelmed by the surprisingly loud roar of ten thousand Watchtower-issued tissue pages shuffling. Malachi! Whhhrrrrrrrrrrrrrr. Revelation! Whrrrrrrrrrr. I flipped frantically to keep up with everyone else, not knowing my Bible as well as they did, my unread pages sticking together more than theirs, which were seasoned by the oils and cells of their fingertips. I most often had to give up, as the verse would have been read before I had even found it. But when he announced the big ones like Matthew, Mark, Luke, and John, I was already expert at finding those.

During one of these talks, between counting the lights on the scoreboard and trying to unstick my Bible pages, something a frail-looking man read bombastically through the crackling speakers arrested my attention. It was about some sheep and some goats. Perhaps because it was surprising to hear about cute animals in the endless reel of four days' worth of words and sentences and pauses and baby cries, or maybe because it reminded me of the illustrations I had seen in those pictures in one of the pink books I had flipped through at Grandma's, my attention was drawn in razor-sharp. I easily found the passage he was reading, in Matthew. And as I read along with him, the ten thousand other people disappeared. It was just me, and God talking to me. I was in a very perilous position. My world began to make sense, and it was being revealed to me through this man in a suit. Turns out, little did I realize until this moment, but hanging out at the odd meeting with Grandma, watching hockey banners—this was not going to cut it. There were sheep, and there were goats. The sheep were going to live, and the goats were going to die, and very soon. And worst of all, I was quite likely going to be one of those people falling into the fiery crevice at Armageddon; I was one of those goats. This was why my grandma was taking us here. We would die if we didn't go. My dad would die, my mom would die . . . my sister definitely, and maybe even my baby brother, too.

I don't know if the other eight-year-olds in the room were thinking what I was thinking. I'm sure the drunk dad at home and the mother who had never really wanted children and had retreated from her unhappy marriage into herself and her bitterness couldn't have helped. But since my scoreboard-light daydreams had caused me to miss out on the most important part of his sermon—that is, how I could be a sheep and thereby not be killed—I felt around below my seat with my arm and quietly ripped a piece of paper off my lunch bag. I placed it in that page of Matthew in the kelp green Bible my grandma had bought at the literature counter for me, to reread later, at home, in my bedroom, away from my parents—goats—who, I had discovered, had raised us as a bunch of goats. And we were all going to die.

Jean and I met for many lunches and walks around Shanghai before I got up the courage to bring up the Bible. I had put it off for quite some time, instead inviting her on bike rides through the winding streets that connected our two worlds, routes framed with the multicolored bark of the London plane trees planted years before by the French, the camaraderie of understanding strengthening between us with each word we taught each other in our respective languages.

I felt like a teenager again, with very little responsibility and a lot of time to explore, my only accountability a number reflecting the hours I had spent doing this filled out on a form at the end of the month and sent off by a brother to our Brooklyn or Hong Kong headquarters, where I was admired for my sacrifice of moving to this closed-off place. I visited Jean at her house, where she cooked green soybeans stir-fried with garlic and chili, and pork with the sweet cabbage of winter. She introduced me to mala hot pot and northern mantou buns, and as we spoke in our hybrid fusion of English and Chinese, we both learned a lot. As the weather became cooler, I brought her to the Western-style coffee shops, where a cappuccino cost more than ordering a dish in a regular restaurant. Jean was extremely open to new things, new foods, and new experiences, and the more I got to know her, the more I got the feeling that she was a humble person who would most likely welcome many of the things I was here to teach her.

Feeling guilty that I hadn't yet given her a chance to learn the truth, I prayed about it and began to look for an "in." Everyone's life had things in it that were wrong, sad, or frustrating. And while Jean was optimistic by nature and shy to share things about herself, finally one day she shared something sad, and I knew that was my cue.

One early evening I met her at a restaurant that she had wanted me to try. It was a beautiful night, and I had taken the side streets, where the other riders seemed to move in slow motion through the dusky air. The restaurant looked very plain from the front, a backlit plastic sign with red Chinese characters that glowed and flashed, while fluorescent lights whitened everything they lit inside. The walls were tiles, and on the tables sat pots of chilis and jars of chopsticks.

We were early and the staff was still eating their own dinner, but they waved us over to another table and the *laoban* (boss), with curler-set hair, placed some laminated menus on the table. Of course, Jean had "*qing*ed" me (literally, said the words "*Wo yao qing ni,*" which means "I want to invite you" but is code for "I am treating you"), which meant that she would not only be treating me but also doing the ordering. After studying the menu a minute, she called the waitress over and ordered the things that she thought I would think were delicious, but left off ordering other dishes that were her favorites, no doubt, because she knew of my aversion to animal entrails.

Jean seemed excited and proud as we waited for the food to come. She told me she was very happy to be able to introduce this style of food to me, as it was from a northern province of China, where the food was spicy and quite different from what one typically found in the South. Of course, Shanghai was a cosmopolitan city, and any style of food could be procured here—the key was knowing where to find it and how to order it, something I would not have been able to do on my own at this early stage in my sojourn. I couldn't even read the restaurant signs very well, let alone know which region's food would suit my fancy. But Jean and I soon found out that our taste in food (any organs aside) was quite compatible—we liked salty, spicy foods, and lots of vegetables. A full meal in these local restaurants often cost no more than $5 or $10 for two people, so we ate out together often.

When the first couple of dishes came to the table, Jean motioned with a hand to the plates and said, "*Qing*." It was my privilege to go first, and I picked a few things and put them on the bowl of rice in front of me.

I asked Jean about how her job was going, and she responded in the positive way she often did, but seemed to be harboring some things that she'd like to say but did not say, as she was not accustomed to complaining. I knew if I asked enough questions, I would learn more. Her British boss seemed worried, and there was trouble in the company. She was the receptionist, which was a job she enjoyed, but what she really longed to do was be a Chinese-language teacher for expats. Immediately after revealing this to me, Jean laughed and shook her head in embarrassment. She was such an unselfish, self-effacing person, on the surface it could seem as if she was timid or insecure. But timid people did not teach themselves English living in a two-room house with five siblings in the country-side, then go off to university and move to Shanghai all on their own. Jean's outer kindness and deference were a layer of goodness that touched all she did. But underlying it, she was a woman with a will of steel, and she had a determination that was not unlike my own, with my drive to come here and convert.

The next dish came, a fish with its head still on. It was deli-cious with chili and sauce. I tried to avert my gaze from its eyes as I ate. Jean and I spoke in Chinese, mainly, so I had to pay very close attention to make sure I was understanding every-thing. Anytime I couldn't, Jean would muster up the confi-dence to tell me what something meant in English. She always knew but would use her English only when she had to, because my Chinese had failed.

Finally, when our meal was nearly finished, and the cooks were having a cigarette before returning to their kitchen out back, Jean told me that she was feeling sad, because her favor-ite grandma had passed away some months ago, and she had not been able to get back to their village in time to see her be-fore she died.

I had begun to enjoy the friendship with her so much that I at times forgot what its premise was. But I had been looking for this "in," and my training was so ingrained that when someone talked about some sadness or difficulty that my beliefs had the ability to ameliorate, the phrases I had learned to master at meetings for my entire life came to my mind automatically. They were awkward in this new tongue, but still they moved like a reflex from my mouth. I seized the opportunity.

"Jean, I am so sorry. It is so hard to accept when a loved one dies." This was what we always said when commenting on a loved one's death, though certainly I did not phrase it so eloquently in Mandarin. I most likely said something that sounded like "I feel bad. That is sad."

"Thank you," Jean said.

Then came the pivot. "Jean, when my dad died, I felt the same way. But there is something that helped me a lot."

"Oh?"

"Yes, and that is, that there is a way that one day, you can see your grandmother again."

I switched halfway through to English, because I really could not say all I needed to say in Chinese.

"I like to read the Bible, and after my dad died it brought me a lot of comfort to know that the Bible says we will see him again. God doesn't forget people when they die, people like your grandmother."

Jean listened graciously. Then she told me that she knew about the Bible. She used to have a friend from America, whom she met at the university. They had celebrated Christmas together and been very close. Then the friend's mother became ill, and the woman had to move back to the United States.

In Jean's mind, I was the same as this woman, a Christian, her friend. To me, the woman sounded like a nice person in a

false religion. I saved for later the conversation about not cele-
brating Christmas because it was pagan, as that would only
complicate things. I asked Jean if the next time we met, I could
bring something to show her what the Bible said about people
who have died.

Of course, Jean agreed. This was what we did in this
friendship—it was built on a foundation of showing each other
the things we liked: foods, coffees, religion, language, and we
were both open to trying them.

When we met the next time, I brought a photocopy of the
chapter of the brochure we used for studying the Bible with
people, the page that talked about God's hope for dead loved
ones. I got to the coffee shop early so that we could have a
booth, for privacy. Jean arrived and I ordered a cappuccino for
both of us, since I was the one doing the inviting this time.

After we chatted, I pulled out the crinkled page. It was written in simplified Chinese, but I had studied this book with
people so many times already in Taiwan that I knew the lines
by heart, even without reading them. Plus, even in the English
version of the brochure, the sentences had been written at a
reading level that even a child could understand. I asked Jean
to read the first paragraph, out loud. Jean took the paper, and
I saw her look at the fuzzy illustration on the right side of the
page, white people in front, crying tears of joy, embracing other
white people: a mother with her child, a father surrounded by
family, then in the back, two black men in traditional African
dress. She then pointed to the paragraph and looked up, asking me if this was where she should start. I pointed, yes. She
began:

Many millions of people who are dead in the grave will return to life on Earth. Even some who did not know God and who practiced bad things will be resurrected.

To me, it sounded like the most wonderful hope. I looked up and noticed that Jean looked a bit perplexed. She was not one to argue, or to voice disagreement to me. But after having read these lines so many times, I was numb to their meaning, and I looked again to try and discern what was wrong. I had only the Chinese character version in front of us, and as I scanned the lines of text, I recognized the characters for "bad" and "people."

I had a difficult time imagining that Jean's grandmother, if she was at all similar to Jean, was someone who practiced "bad things."

I wondered if that was what Jean was thinking about, and I backtracked a bit:

"Of course, there are so many good people who have died, too, who just never got the chance to learn what God wanted them to do."

Jean smiled at me and adjusted her glasses, turning the page over to see if anything was written on the back.

"Oh. I see. Yes, I have always wanted to learn more about the Bible. I think Christians are good people."

"Yes, there are lots of good things in the Bible that can make our life better," I said. I promised to bring the next chapter the next time we met, and then I could show her more.

I had my first friend here, and now, my first Bible student.

Though Jean had always wanted to be a teacher, I felt the opposite, maybe because all I did was teach, between the English tutoring and the Bible students. There were not that many work opportunities overseas for someone like me: no degree, only willing to work part-time, and with no specific profession. But being a foreigner in Asia, there were other forms of work to be had. I tried editing movie subtitles created by a bot for a while. In Taiwan, I had acted as an extra in a TV series and starred in a laundry detergent ad (this was not a pretty sight—I avoided all televisions for months to avoid seeing myself act). Nothing really stuck until one day I found work that used the one area of expertise I had: Chinese. After studying Mandarin and interacting so closely with my Chinese Bible students and the Taiwanese brothers and sisters for years, if there was one thing (besides the Bible) I was well versed in, it was Chinese culture, and my Mandarin was getting to the point where I could use it in a job.

The first time I had ever heard a podcast was in Taiwan. It was 2005, and podcasts were the latest of the new media that were taking over the Internet. Three Western businessmen had started a small company in a building in a back alley of Shanghai whose mission was to teach Mandarin by podcast. Someone had told me about the shows when I was in Taiwan, and I had listened to a few of them. This was a new way of learning a language, to download these lessons to an iPod and listen to shows with hosts who became like friends. When I moved to Shanghai, I dreamed of working there instead of teaching English. I was much more interested in Mandarin than I was in my mother tongue.

After some time in Shanghai, I decided to write to the company, ChinesePod, to ask if they might need someone to help. I told them I could translate and was willing to do anything. They did need help, as it happened, and asked me to come in to the studio the next week. We talked about what I could do for them, and I was hired shortly after, to work three days a week translating lessons from Mandarin to English, doing general quality checks on the site, and helping with the online community. Facebook and other social media barely existed at this point (it was 2006), but groups with common interests had started forming chat groups on websites or through LISTSERV. The ChinesePod website had an online forum with lots of active users—most of them people who were foreigners learning Chinese for one reason or another. I kept my cover as a vague "person interested in China" with my bosses and workmates and, because it was part of my work, began to emerge into the digital world through the thick walls of this country where, if you wrote the wrong combination of keywords, your website could be shut down.

My new work visa was processed quickly because of someone's connections somewhere, and from my first day, I was thrilled with the job. As a Witness, I had never been in a creative environment like this and did not know that one could earn money doing something so interesting and enjoyable. As a child, I had often played with a mic my dad had brought home, plugging it into the JVC stereo and hitting the red circle record button to make radio programs on a cassette tape. I loved speaking into a microphone, and though I hated the sound of my voice, I loved going back in time to moments earlier, hearing the thump of the cassette wheels moving, seeing the slow motion of the tape unreeling to the sounds of my commentary, no audience to judge me but myself. The whole enterprise was tantalizing. But, of course, I was just a part-time translator—not one of the hosts, who were the stars of the podcasts—and had no idea how to get to there from where I was.

The man I had heard on that first podcast, back when I was in Taiwan, was the company's big star—a dark-haired, handsome man in his early thirties from Oklahoma, named Aric with an *A*. He had a deep, alluring radio voice. He would roll in on Fridays to record Saturday's show, having been all but fired from the job after some conflict with one of the bosses, hanging by the last string of his charm and listenership, and I would watch him from the corner of my eye, curious. My only interaction with him thus far at the company was an attempt to actively avoid him by hiding in the staircase one day when he asked me to be in the company Christmas video. Everyone on the team was taking turns recording a holiday greeting for a video he was going to cut together and post on the message boards for the podcast's fans. I panicked and knew I could not appear on such a video, as a Witness. It was like I was back in high school all over again—spoken to by the cool person, for once, only to have to reconfirm to him just how uncool I was.

No one made a big deal that I wasn't on the video, thankfully, but a few months later Aric decided he wanted to do a podcast episode that he said would be the *Sex and the City* of Shanghai. He asked me and two other women who worked in the office if he could have us on the show to talk about what it was like to be a foreign woman in Shanghai.

I was thrilled, but again there were a few problems. One, I had never seen a single episode of *Sex and the City*. I had been out of North America for quite some time by this point, and while we could buy entire series of any show we wanted in the back-alley markets for a few dollars, no Witness would touch anything that had the word *sex* in the title. Another problem was that I was married and did not go out much at all, so I was not really qualified to speak to what the "scene" was like in Shanghai. The third big problem was that I was a missionary doing illegal work in China and supposed to keep a low profile. Being on this podcast that nearly every foreigner in China was listening to hardly qualified. I was meant to be invisible.

All the same, I wanted to be on the show, and after having hidden from the Christmas video, I could not dodge Aric this time without outing myself as a total freak. As fortune would have it, I did not have to reveal much on the show about myself, because for one thing, Aric was the star and talked much of the time. But for another, my vocal cords were so constricted in nervousness that when I did speak, the words barely came out.

Still, when the episode aired, I listened and scoured the comments section for people's thoughts on it. Even though it might have been an activity I could have gotten in trouble for, I was still very interested.

A month or so after that, another chance came, due to a combination of sick days and a small, start-up-size staff. The host of one of the Mandarin learning shows called "Qing Wen" (a podcast that answered people's questions about tricky parts of Chinese grammar) couldn't make it in for the recording. The episodes were on a strict schedule and had to be made available on their usual days without fail, so Ken, the cohost of the show (and our boss), asked me if I would like to fill in. It was short notice, so there wasn't as much time to get nervous, and Ken was a kind, warm older Irishman with a paunch— hardly as intimidating as Aric. Along with us for the recording was my favorite Chinese colleague, Connie. I prepared for the lesson by looking at what they planned to discuss and was in the recording studio within the hour. The sound engineer gave us the go-ahead, and my voice came out (thankfully). I had fun, and the lesson went well. After that, they let me fill in, from time to time, as a substitute host for the show.

Meanwhile, at the end of each of my workdays, I left the studio and hopped on my bike, vanishing back into my secret world. My routines continued as they had been—I looked for Bible students, went to meetings on the weekend, and hung out with some of the other Witnesses who were also in Shanghai.

None of the Witnesses I knew from the meetings asked me about my job—we weren't really focused on what people did for a living—except for my two closest friends, Emma and Rosemary, who had also begun to listen to the shows, because they learned so much from them. We talked about the podcasts as we walked around the city preaching together, or over Chinese foot massages. I told them how the lessons were made and what the stars of the show were like, and we talked about what other lessons would be helpful to people learning Mandarin.

While the podcast work was nothing of importance in comparison to what we did on our days off—going around the city, saving people—we were all excited about this new way of learning a language, and I had for the first time felt what it was like to make something and be proud of it.

Emma and I met up to go out preaching once a week or so. By now, I had three or four regular Bible students whom I had cultivated, including Jean, and I corresponded with many "potentials" over text, making plans or just saying hello and being friendly so that I could start counting my preaching time. One day, after texting one of these "potentials," Emma and I decided to head to IKEA and have meatballs and bottomless coffee while we looked for a friendly-seeming Chinese person we could strike up a conversation with. It was fun to hang out at IKEA and catch up, seeing as most of what we talked about we couldn't say over the phone or on the Internet, in case the authorities were listening.

Plus, IKEA was a perfect place for preaching. We didn't stand out much—meatballs being the great unifier of palates in the world—and the familiar Swedish surroundings made the store an attractive prospect to most Westerners living in China. The cafeteria was one of the rare places where it was natural for foreigners to share a table with a local person. Also, because it was a private business, there was less chance of spies.

That may sound a little dramatic, but before the weather had gotten so hot, I had met for study sessions in Renmin Park. One day I noticed two men in polyester suits snapping photos of me and my Bible student. I quickly got up to leave, telling my student to go in another direction, and I decided that being in such an open place as a foreigner with a local might not be the best idea anymore.

After an hour or so of eating lunch, chatting, scanning the room, and deliberating choosing a spot next to people who seemed like friendly-looking targets, I decided I better try to approach someone, if I was to continue counting time for this. I was low on my preaching hours for the month, because I now worked in the "real" world more than most pioneers did.

I went up to the coffee and tea area to refill my cup, hoping it would help me summon some courage. A woman with silver-threaded black hair, about forty-eight years old, dressed in jeans and a thin polyester tunic popular with those of her generation, was beside me. As I placed my cup on the rubber pad and pulled the handle of the coffee dispenser, she glanced up at me in surprise for a few seconds, her eyes going from me to the cup, then back downward. She returned to her task of removing a large number of sugar packets and powdered coffee creamer pouches from a plastic bin onto a plastic tray that held her customized IKEA travel mug filled with hot water. I watched my coffee cup fill with the black liquid, a little swirl of oil licking its surface, and used the time to muster the energy it took me to approach a stranger. I looked at her and said hello in Chinese. Not noticing that I was speaking her language, she laughed nervously and pointed at the dispenser, pulling out the sugar for me as a sort of offering. *"Bu yao, bu yao,"* I said, which meant "Don't want, don't want" (this phrase sounds a lot ruder in English than it does in Chinese). She put a handful on my tray. "Is free," she said, educating me in the ways of the place.

I thanked her. Then, bumbling, I asked her, for lack of anything better to say, "You like coffee?"

"No, no, just hot water," she said, in Chinese. "Your Chinese is so fluent!"

"No, no, it's nothing," I said.

She moved to carry her tray back to her table and I walked somewhat awkwardly alongside her. She seemed not to mind my being there, but there's no doubt it was unusual for a young foreign woman to want to interact with a middle-aged Shanghainese woman. Looking around, there wasn't one table where a Chinese person and a Western person were sharing proximity by choice, rather than by the circumstance of too many people and not enough tables.

When we got near her table, I asked her if my friend and I could sit with her. The cafeteria seating was crowded, and she and her friend had clearly done their best to pile belongings and trays such that they could have the table to themselves. Even so, she enthusiastically agreed, inviting me in a manner no less hospitable than if I were coming to her home for refreshments of hot water and sugar. When I looked up, Emma was watching me, and I waved her over. As she arrived at the table, I introduced her, and she tentatively gave a little wave and greeting. The woman told us her name was Xiao Li. It seemed like a nickname, its literal meaning being "small" Li, but I couldn't be sure. Her friend, slightly older and thinner than Xiao Li, was called Yan; she was entertaining an infant wearing thin white cotton mittens. She introduced the baby she was holding as her grandchild.

Since the women's first language was Shanghainese, which is a dialect, rather than an official language people learned in school, their Mandarin was heavily accented, and at first I struggled to understand them. After some trial and error, I deciphered that they lived just behind the IKEA, square in its shadow. They each had lived in their homes for their entire married lives, in a hutong alley, long before IKEA and foreigners came to this part of town. Their homes had no air-conditioning and were falling apart to some degree, they said, so when the giant yellow structure began to rise floor by floor, displacing a chunk of their neighbors with it, they had felt somewhat alarmed. That is, until the store opened, and they realized that this Western store would allow them to sit in the cool, clean cafeteria all day long, all year long, enjoying bottomless coffee and free sugar, and that's exactly what they did. They came nearly every day, they told me; it was like the comfortable living room they had never had. It wouldn't be much longer now, though, Xiao Li explained, because the government was going to tear down the hutong and move them out to another area, far outside the city center. I asked them how they felt about leaving their homes. They said it was fine because they were told everything would be new, even the appliances. But that they would miss the desserts at IKEA, even if they were too sweet.

These two ladies seemed perfectly harmless to preach to,

and though in my experience women their age in Shanghai weren't usually interested in discussions about the Bible, I felt it was important to give everyone a chance at responding to the good news. But still, it was too soon to let them know our motive. We'd have to try and meet again and steer the conversation to find out what their husbands did for work, and whether anyone in the family was a Communist Party member.

Emma and I stayed there for a while with them. Eventually we ran out of things to talk about, and they were struggling a bit to understand our English-accented Chinese. I was almost sure this was the first time they had heard their language botched in this manner. We exchanged numbers so that we could text each other and told them we'd come by again next week on our trip to IKEA. They seemed surprised but happy, and told us they'd be here. We said our "*zaijians*" (which means "goodbye") and sauntered through the furniture staging area. A man was napping on one of the display beds we passed.

Now the question was: Where to go next? It was sweltering, ninety-seven degrees and 100 percent humidity. The air-conditioning at IKEA had been turned up to an arctic setting, and the heat was smothering when we got outside. I was thankful to be warm, but I wondered how Xiao Li and her friend could acclimatize back to the temperatures of their homes at night when they had to reluctantly leave the store to get their husbands' dinners ready. Did they dream of having not only air-conditioning but also a living room and kitchen like the ones they passed on their way out? Of a new mattress with prettily patterned sheets? Hopefully in their new housing, they would have all this and more.

I pulled my scraped-up white bike free of the tangle of spokes and pedals and pushed it toward Emma, who was putting her lock under her seat. I leaned back, my skirt taut against the bike's bar under it. We decided to ride toward Renmin Park. There was an underground mall where Emma had talked to a couple of shop owners a few weeks before, and at least it would be somewhat cooler down there than outside.

There was a break in the bike traffic and we pulled out into the bike lane, not wearing helmets because no one wore them—except Mormons, who were known in Taiwan as the "helmet preachers." Here on the Mainland, people probably didn't know the difference yet, but the last thing we wanted was to be mistaken for Mormons; we didn't want to stand out as Bible thumpers, and anyhow, we considered ourselves to be the cooler cousin of the other religions here on missionary tours.

The sweat had already started to trickle down my back and above my ears by the time we reached Xujiahui, ten or so blocks away. The French Concession was right after that, with its large, leafy trees, narrow streets, and cooler shade.

My preaching days were spent like this. Time flew by until the next workday came, when I would unlock my bike in the morning and pedal fast to get to Huangpi Road, stopping for a *jianbing* from the street vendor and carrying it in its thin plastic bag into the elevator, bidding a good morning to the old man who sat reading his Chinese translation of *Men Are from Mars, Women Are from Venus* between operating the manual elevator that went up to the office.

Much as the lady in IKEA had praised my Chinese, foreigners who attempt to speak Chinese in China are often praised for their language abilities, even if their Chinese isn't that good. How to receive these compliments appropriately was one of the many linguistic situations that an English speaker would inevitably discover—once they were far enough into learning the language to even understand a compliment—had no direct equivalent in English or Chinese.

Our Chinese teachers and the textbooks we used often gave Chinese versions of the English phrases used for circumstances like this, but Westerners just could not wrap their minds around what was culturally appropriate for their listeners, rather than for themselves. After a long enough time in China, I noticed that no Chinese people ever actually used many of these phrases we had been taught. I wondered why there often seemed to be no direct translation for the ways our language helped us convey humility, greetings, or sentiment.

This was not because of a lack of words or expressions available that had an equivalent meaning. Rather it was because of the very different ways Westerners and Chinese people had of seeing others and the world. Learning Chinese was not only about learning grammar and memorizing vocabulary. It also involved excavating your head and learning an entirely new way of thinking about things.

For example, as English speakers, it was so ingrained in our culture to greet others with an inquiry after their well-being ("How are you?"), we couldn't accept that there was no direct Chinese equivalent. Collectively, the Chinese teachers of the world seemed to have buckled under our demands and written the literal equivalent of *"Ni hao ma?"* (translates as: You good, question mark?) into the textbooks. Chinese people seemed to get it when we said it, or were good at pretending we were making sense, out of politeness. But after a couple of years, no one had yet answered my query after their well-being in a satisfying way (by saying, for example, "Fine"). Most often when the question was posed it was returned with a nervous laugh or nodding of the head; at times, a *"Ni hao, ni hao"* ("Hello," or literally "You good") in return.

I never realized all of this until one day when one of my Bible students felt comfortable enough with me to inform me that the way Westerners responded to compliments was strange. Or that asking how a person "was" as a way to open a conversation was weird. Chinese people didn't show interest or concern in the same way we did. Instead, they'd state the obvious, or something they had observed, to open an exchange: "You just came back from the market." Or "You're going to work." Or "You look tired." Or, as one student learning English told me in the morning, "You've lost weight!" and another that same afternoon, "You've put on weight!" What had actually happened was that I had gotten a haircut.

It's possible that this was because in China, you just saw so many people in one day, it was too much to deal with if you asked about everyone's well-being. After a number of years facing down the thousands upon thousands of people I'd see in a day, I did not want to know how each of them was feeling either. Also, if a person here was to inquire after one's well-being, they would do it by asking if they had eaten yet, to show concern. I was never offered food when I said no, but then when I asked, "How are you?," I never really thought about whether the person was okay or not, did I?

On the other hand, even though no one inquired about your state of being, there were many questions asked of a very personal nature. For example, the top five questions that a new acquaintance might ask would often include:

— How old are you?
— How much money do you make?
— Do you have a girlfriend (or boyfriend)?
— Why don't you have any children?

And if you were pudgy at all:

— How much do you weigh?

Almost any of which would be considered grievously rude in our cultures, and possibly cause a lot of discomfort.

How differently one had to think in order to function in this society became evident to the foreigner early. Seemingly mundane tasks turned into perplexing challenges. For example, sending a letter: Where Westerners write addresses from the conceptually smallest part of the address to biggest (starting at the individual, with the person's name, and ending at the country), Chinese people address their letters starting at the country and ending with the person. When Westerners state our names, we start from our given name and end with our surname. In China, it's the opposite. This was a symptom of a greater cultural difference. Where in the West, the matters of life revolved around the individual, in China, the individual was subject to the greater structures they were a part of. Family and country came first, just as they did on their envelopes and in their names.

There was also the minefield of what was lucky or unlucky. To us, the concepts of luck or unluckiness were childish things of cats and ladders. But in China, luck is taken very seriously, and unluckiness, even more so. Certain numbers, those that sounded similar phonetically to the Chinese word meaning "death," could produce a severe level of anxiety, especially given that foreigners have difficulty with a major feature of the Chinese language: when you change your intonation, you change the meaning of a word. So while a new student of Chinese may have thought they were innocently saying they wanted to go to the fourth floor, they could actually have been telling someone about their death. And this is a culture where talking about death is a serious taboo.

Other things that seemed like nice gestures—for example, presenting an item as a gift that, unknown to you, was unlucky—

could be scandalous. When one older Witness friend brought Jean a clock for a housewarming gift (after noticing that she used her cell phone as her alarm clock), Jean's roommate let out an audible gasp as the wrapping paper was peeled back. In Chinese, a language full of homonyms, the phrase "give a clock" sounded exactly like the phrase for attending another's funeral, thus rendering the gift completely taboo. What were the odds that someone would choose a clock—the worst possible gift—as a present? It's not as if clocks were common presents! But this was how it happened, and at times it felt like almost anything that you did without thinking—or whenever you did what seemed like the natural thing to do in your culture—turned out to be the thing you should have thought a little more about.

Then there were the matters of health—on hot days, when I would arrive at a Bible student's home, they would set out hot water to drink. They were horrified by the idea of ice in water, which according to Chinese medicine was the worst thing one could do to cool oneself down, not to mention that it would age you or cause all kinds of disruption to bodily systems. And related to that, where a Westerner considered skin too pale to be a sign of sickness, and a tan the sign of a healthy glow, almost all of the women I knew in China avoided the sun and used whitening creams. One particularly transparent-looking young woman I met once told me that she had never been in the sun in her entire life.

The beds were hard—not firm-mattress hard, but hard-as-a-board hard—and furniture was often made of wood, with few or no cushions. The houses and buildings rarely had central heat and were most often lit by cold, fluorescent lighting, which was considered modern and clean as opposed to the soft, incandescent mood lighting I liked, which to them was reminiscent of old-fashioned village life. The Chinese believed in showering at night, and I had shocked more than one friend when they found out that I would go to bed without bathing first. For my part, I wondered at how this wasn't a nation full of bedhead, what with everyone going to sleep with wet hair.

Or the differences in what constituted good manners—when inviting a guest to a restaurant, to me the most hospitable and generous thing would be to say "Order whatever you want!" But in China, the most hospitable thing you could do was order all the best dishes for your dining guest, saving them from any deliberation in the matter, like when Jean had treated me in the northern Chinese food restaurant. And on the related matter of eating, though we are accustomed to having drinks with our meal, restaurants in China generally have no beverages; you had to go to the convenience store next door if you wanted even bottled water. To order your food, or ask for the bill, you shout for the waitress. She won't come until you do. And you have to shout loud, because meals, even in fancy restaurants, are a boisterous affair.

Parks are not peaceful places either, in general. "*Renao*" is a concept you learn about early on in China, used to describe a place bustling with clamor and crowds. Chinese people like their public spaces to be noisy, full of excitement and energy at all times. I once lived next to a park, and early each morning the older people of the neighborhood would drag a KTV machine, replete with generator, to sing songs on the microphone, turned up loud. Or someone would bring out a boom box and play music, from ballroom to techno, and people would dance to it. In the nicer parks, it is not unusual to see twenty or so men in light blue or gray suits, and women in rented and pinned dresses, taking their wedding pictures. In one park I saw a bucking bronco machine. You get used to action.

Though I am a relatively set-in-my-routines kind of person, I eventually gave in to doing things like everyone else around me, regardless of how I would have done it at home. I drank warm water on hot days. I left my bike locked to its own tire, not to a rack or pole. I wore no seat belt in the car, and it felt just fine (when it most probably was not fine at all).

Learning this language and living in this world required a U-turn of the mind. It required seeing the world with a refracted understanding. And when I understood more about what was behind the Chinese view of person versus country, and person versus family—which was really about a human being's place in the world—I came to understand a logic that had developed completely independently of the logic of the West that I had always taken as a given. And though the Chinese way of thinking was at times completely opposite of what made sense to me instinctually, it made perfect sense all on its own.

It was a different way of being in the world. I was in a mild state of disorientation for a number of years, and one of the unexpected effects was that I was slowly made a little less sure that the world was in fact as I had always seen it.

Disorientation is kryptonite to a preacher. For the preacher, uncertainty cannot exist. It is the preacher whose job it is to proclaim, to make known a thing that she knows without doubt. The preacher, unlike the teacher, asks no questions of herself, as she already has the answer.

There is no human so bold as the preacher. Or so blind. For they do all the talking, and none of the asking.

f I was the preacher, Jean was a model adherent. She treated my words with a reverence, as if they were an opening into a world she had curiosity about but no access to. Her drive to learn English came from a thirst to learn, and this trait had not withered as she matured. I had what she needed.

As we studied she never once hinted at any doubts she may have had about my teachings. She never questioned anything I said. And while she learned the words for "God," "Jesus," and "Armageddon" as I taught them to her in Chinese, they were not words of her language. If she did not believe, if she doubted what I taught her, she did not say, as the student may not allow the instructor to lose face. And this was exactly what the preacher sought. To tell, not to hear.

We were the perfect vehicle to meet each other's needs. She developed a taste for the cappuccinos I bought her, and I developed a taste for the pu'er tea she poured for me.

But as time went by, I began to notice that without her even trying to teach me anything, I had begun to learn from Jean. She would share a teaching of Confucius that applied to what we were learning, beginning out of excitement, but then cutting herself off at her rudeness. I stopped and asked her more. She taught me that many of the Christian qualities the Bible encouraged were the same as those encouraged in Confucian thought—goodness and benevolence, fairness, loyalty, cooperation, compassion. Many of the moral values Confucius held out were the same as those encouraged in the Bible. Both even had a "golden rule" (though theirs was sometimes called silver). I felt surprised that the same wisdom could be drawn from such different places.

Sometimes the conclusions were different as well, but the teachings of Laozi that she shared made as much sense to me as those of Moses or Paul. She loved to tell me what the four-word Chinese idioms (*chengyu*) meant when you pulled them apart. I thought to myself many times: what a good preacher she will make, when she is ready.

We began to spend as much time talking about other things as we did about the Bible. We both enjoyed our study but also looked forward to the moment the chapter was finished and our books were put discreetly back into our bags, and our other conversations could begin.

What had started with Jean had also begun to wedge itself in my other Bible studies. When I gave them their copies of our publications and a Bible, the covers carefully wrapped so as not to alert any around us to their content, I had felt as though I was a bestower of truth, a giver of happiness and the peace of mind I had myself. I was convinced I could save them, here in the noisy corner of a McDonald's or on the bench of a shopping mall. But as my Chinese improved, I began to notice that the people I studied with were reacting in ways I hadn't picked up on before I understood the culture and language to the degree I did now. Occasionally, I would feel a flush of embarrassment, as I sensed a shift in tone as the student across the table read through a paragraph in the book:

> As soon as Jesus became King, he threw Satan and his wicked angels out of heaven and down to the locality of the Earth. That is why things have become so bad here on earth since 1914.

"1914?" The date seemed to get larger, and weirder, the longer we stared at it on the page. This date had been a given in my life, and its significance as the beginning of the end times was beyond question for me, and in fact there was a whole chain of scriptures I had written down from one of our publications that I could use to prove its truth. But as we read through the paragraphs and talked about the pictures in the book, it occurred to me that some of this seemed to my students quaint, or silly even. A look or a pause would reveal to me that some of the things that I had taken as lifelong truths, things that I had built my life around, seemed just crazy to them. At times I would cringe inside when I noticed that what I said could have been insulting—perhaps even arrogant. The things I taught as universal truths completely disregarded the lived experience of much of the world's population. Creation? One God? Everlasting life? Stay away from worldly family members? Marry in the lord (there was no one in the lord to marry here!)? Don't care about money? Don't get an education?

They would sometimes laugh a little, especially at this last idea.

As I read to them from the Bible, I myself began to wonder about what was going on in the world outside of the Middle East in the same era, counting back in the timeline of Chinese history to figure out what was happening in Asia when Jesus was flinging Satan out of heaven or curing the sick.

Still, I taught them that this religion I told them about was the chosen one, better than all the others—so-called Christian religions, Buddhism, Islam, Daoism, Mormonism—all of them. I did so without question as to the veracity of my conviction. But what I did wonder about was why my conviction in my rightness was any less valid than that of any other true believer. Why had God made it such that some people, like me, grew up in a society that revolved around Christianity, and others in one that revolved around entirely different, yet equally moral, systems of belief? And what was the price for that everlasting destruction (if they didn't listen to me)? If my religion was the only one that God accepted, why hadn't God made it a more level playing field?

I wanted to believe—had always believed—that the truth was simple. I was starting to understand that truth was ambiguous, and subjective. So much of who we are is what we have been taught by our culture, or even our family. Why did God make us such complicated beings, and why couldn't he make the important things that a human race might need to know more evident—say, with an address from the clouds every Friday afternoon to remind us of why we were here and how we were supposed to live? Why did he suddenly vanish, after a few appearances here in the Bible? Was he purposely trying to obfuscate? Really, where was he at all?

Though I had started to question myself, my relationships with my Bible students had started on this foot, and it wasn't up to me to upend them. These people wanted something from me, and surely what they wanted was to be saved. And I didn't know how else to interact with people; preaching was all I had ever done. It was who I was.

Not one of them quit studying with me. They began inviting me to dinners in giant restaurants with their families and colleagues, dishing out the choicest cuts of meat into my bowl. So I preached on, realizing that it was difficult to find any other comfortable place in a dynamic that had formed within a certain premise. And because, despite my occasional misgivings, I was sure that everything I learned, on the whole, added up, and that was what mattered. There was no way this world was going to go on like this. Someone had to save us.

Sooner or later, in the course of a Bible study, my students and I would get to the climax of the book: the chapter on Armageddon. There, with its two-page centerfold illustration of fire falling from the sky, people dying, reeling into the gaping earth, I would explain these things to them. I had done it for years, to anyone who would listen, happy at being able to show them the truth. And now I started to hear what I was saying, for the first time:

"So, you see, because you were born here, and I was born into my world, God is going to kill you and your family and friends and associates, but not me. Because you were educated differently, in a different culture, and therefore have a different explanation for life, for spirituality, for goodness, for meaning . . . you will die, and I will live. This is because I was taught week in, week out, from the time I was a child, that this all made perfect sense. And you, sadly, were not. Open book to Armageddon centerfold.

"But if you listen to me, you will not die."

I wanted so badly to save people. I needed all of this to be true. I was so desperate for it to be true that I left my home and learned this language and found these people, ignoring any risk that that might mean for them or for me, dismissing the cues that told me I was wrong to be here, that they didn't need me.

I came each week, texted them each morning to start my time, rode my bike in the choking exhaust, flew to the other side of the world, and spent all my time preaching because I could not live with the idea that there were no answers. That everything was not going to be okay. That someone was not going to kill off the "bad" ones. I could not tolerate the idea that one day, I would die, like everyone else.

Yet I found myself asking my students what they thought, now. "Where do Chinese people think that humans came from?" I would ask, comparing notes. "What do you think happens when we die?"

I asked these things for the first time not as a means to figure out how to overcome their objections and show them a better way, as I had done in the past with anyone willing to sit across a table and look at a book with me. But rather to learn what conclusions their six thousand years of human culture had brought them to. Out of genuine curiosity.

Curiosity is a bad quality for the preacher. You preach because you are sure. You preach to people who don't need to hear it, because possibly you are the one who needs to be saved.

t's not surprising that my salvation would come in the form of a man.

After all, a man created me. A man died for my sins. Eight men at Watchtower headquarters told me what kind of man I should marry, and how I ought to spend my time. The man I married was in charge of me, and the men in the congregation delivered sermons to me each week at the Kingdom Hall. Men wrote the books I read. Men told me I should let the men in the congregation do the speaking, and that I should wear long skirts. Three men sat in judgment of me when I confessed to sin (with a man, naturally), and deemed whether I was repentant enough to be allowed to speak to my family and friends. When I wasn't, three men sat in judgment a year later when I begged to be let back in.

I was at work one day when a man wrote me an e-mail. He was one of our podcast listeners and had just had his first Chinese lesson with one of our teachers over Skype. I had helped him coordinate the lesson with the teacher, and he wrote to tell me how it had gone:

From: Jonathan

To: Amber Scorah; Calla Gao

Friday, June 8, 2007 12:20 p.m.

Subject: video of Calla & Taipan's first Chinese lesson

That's me riding the bike. That's my teacher Calla driving the ChinesePod bus.

Zhoumo yukuai.

—Taipan

He had linked to a YouTube video taken by CCTV cameras in a city in the province of Shandong. It recorded a man riding a wobbling bike. He darts out into the street, directly in the path of a bus. A fraction of a second later, the man is hit by the vehicle and pulled underneath its front bumper, disappearing into what looks like certain gore and death.

A crowd gathers, and the fuzzy surveillance video blurs and clears in jittery fits and starts. A few seconds go by, and the bus driver comes down the steps of the vehicle, his movements leaden, to see what carnage he has caused.

After a morbid pause, a horizontal line flickers across the screen, and out from under the bus a man's arm thrusts forward, pulling the body miraculously still connected to it around the bus wheel and onto the sidewalk, where he flops to a stop. The crowd that has gathered is too stunned to move. The video goes to black.

"That's me riding the bike," the e-mail said. And his teacher was driving the bus.

Not a bad analogy for what it feels like to learn Chinese.

Taipan was Jonathan's ChinesePod handle on the discussion boards (lots of students and participants didn't use their actual names in the community conversations). Jonathan was one of the first listeners to our podcasts, and as I would later learn, he was an American who had gone to school years ago at Cornell and had minored in Mandarin—one of the courses of study which at that time tended to be the choice of someone who didn't know what they wanted to do with their life.

He took five years to graduate, moved to Los Angeles, and eventually became a nightclub manager. His only company, for years, was the moody stretch of the nighttime, populated by the people who dwelt in the after-hours belly of a city built for the day. This all until one day, around age thirty, he had an epiphany during a mushroom trip and it came to him that his destiny was to be a writer. He had a friend who was a psychic and had prophesied that Jonathan would become a millionaire (in the 1990s that sounded like a lot more money), and he didn't see himself getting near to fulfilling that divination anytime soon in a nightclub. So he woke up the next Monday to daylight, quit his nighttime job, and enrolled in a screenwriting class, of which there was no shortage in Los Angeles. What he lacked in originality of purpose, he made up for in sheer hard work.

The life of a nighttime careerist lent itself to being distant from others. But his new vocation separated him from close relationships in other ways. He said he had to be secret about what he was writing, since there were thousands of screenwriters in this city and some of them were not shy about swiping ideas or stealing credit.

And while this work, unlike the old work, had a place in the
waking hours of daytime creatures—a hello and a chat with
the barista here, a walk with the dog and greeting to the neighbor there—it was still a natural fit for someone who loved
people as long as they were kept at bay.

Coincidentally, this profession was also perfectly suited to a
relationship over the Internet with a woman he had never met,
whose day started when he had a few minutes in front of the
computer at the dusky time of night when a cool loneliness
crept in with the night desert air, and whose voice could talk
him to sleep at night via language lesson podcasts.

Of course, none of this had been his aim. Wanting to brush
up on his Chinese after all these years, he had signed up for
the online tutoring sessions ChinesePod made available to its
Mandarin-learning customers. The e-mail about the bus was
sent to me after his first lesson. It was a comic metaphor: His
Chinese tutor was the bus driver. He was the guy crawling out
from under the bus.

I burst out laughing after watching the video.

My workmate Clay glanced at me but went back to his
usual flurry of lesson checking and uploading with a furrowed
brow.

I wrote him back right away.

He responded with another e-mail within minutes. Where
did he live? I wondered. All I knew was this screen name he
used, Taipan, and his avatar image—a photo of a squirrel standing up with huge genitals. Seemed like a weird, funny guy.

All of this was normal procedure. I always wrote back to
our listeners. These were the days just before the birth of social

media, and our online forum was full of conversation. The listeners felt like we were their friends, and we tried to get to know them, too. Podcasting was a new medium, this was its first wave, and it was like the whole world was poised, ready to talk to strangers. I talked to nerds in England, men waiting for their arranged-marriage brides in America, expats and English teachers stationed in interior Chinese cities with eight million inhabitants, cities that the Chinese considered small.

Of course, the people I was writing to were worldly people, and while a professional e-mail was one thing, getting too friendly with worldly people was not a good idea. As a Jehovah's Witness, anyone's friendship with a worldly person, other than with the aim of converting them, was frowned upon, because you might be influenced, you might lose your faith if you got close to someone in Satan's world. My husband had already warned me about my job, because I seemed to be enjoying it too much, and often did work after hours, responding to people on the discussion boards. But online media was so new that the Witnesses' Governing Body, who interpreted the Bible into rules that could be applied to modern life, hadn't really covered this situation yet. And at work I was officially not a Jehovah's Witness, because I couldn't let anyone know that preaching was my main reason for being in China, and why I could speak Chinese.

But I wasn't thinking about all of this. I was thousands of miles away from this Taipan, well out of harm's way.

He signed off around 10:30 a.m. my time, to go to bed, after sending me an e-mail with a photo of his night view. He told me he lived in Los Angeles. I didn't know the city well, but his home appeared to be perched high on a hillside; I could see the stripe of a sunset that was on its way to my side of the planet—a neon orange lid sealing in the rectangle lights of a cozy week-night evening in my old time zone, between us the twelve hours of lost time I would never recover until I moved back to North America. I could feel the stillness through the photo, could almost smell the fragrant night. It was something that was out of another Earth for me, one that was easy to forget among the clangs and lights of my neighbors in their buildings that blocked out the color when the sun fell in Shanghai. I missed sunsets.

He would go to bed early, most nights, he explained, because he also ran a yoga studio and had to teach the early class. I wondered if this man could become any more of a cliché. I got busy at work and forgot to reply to his good night, and after looking longingly at the view of a world Shanghai had the ability to erase for me, I didn't think about him for the rest of the day.

Every time I'd arrive at the office now, I'd see a message from Jonathan in my work e-mail account, written in the dead air of pre-smartphone e-mail, brightly backlit letters sent by the sun between his dawn and mine.

Usually they were funny, and I couldn't help but reply with something funny back. He told me about his last lesson, or he asked me a question about Chinese, or mentioned something that someone was talking about on our forum, a question someone had asked overnight that needed a reply.

I was walking a dangerous line, I knew, but I told myself that this was part of my job. And anyway, there were so many layers between Jonathan and me—a screen, a pseudonym, the great firewall of China, even—that it seemed a safe enough distance to write back once, twice, ten times, then answer the Gchat that sprang up in the corner of my screen a couple of weeks later. The lines of staying away from the world were blurrier now, because my preaching now mainly consisted of making friends with worldly people, of hanging out and getting to know them. This made talking to Jonathan seem slightly less wrong than it would have back home; the strict rules about "worldly" association came less readily to mind. Our conversations were still mainly about Chinese lessons, but they were now also creeping into other topics.

We talked about why each of us was studying Chinese. Of course, I had become accustomed to lying about this, and gave him my usual story—that I was from Vancouver, where there were many Chinese immigrants, and I had become entranced with the culture and language after making friends (also known as attempting to convert people to my religion), and had eventually decided that if I was going to really learn the language, I would need to be immersed in it.

His secrecy about certain aspects of his life was akin to my own; we made a fine pair of clandestine correspondents, and for a long time, he told me very few details about himself. I, too, hid so much, it didn't seem strange that he should be able to as well. After I asked enough of the right questions, though, I found out that he was a writer, for film, but he did not reveal more than that. He lived alone, except for the dog he had rescued one night after finding it hurt and wandering alongside the road. Because he didn't seem to do much else other than work, and talk to me, he mostly enjoyed hearing about what I had done in the twenty-four hours since we last spoke, what had happened on the other side of the ocean while he slept, in this world he had never seen.

And something had always happened. Having twenty million people around me meant there wasn't a day where there wasn't some incident, some theft, some interesting thing that I had seen, some delicious food, or something I had learned and could share with him. I had not yet seen a picture of this man, but in a religion obsessed with bodily pureness, the absence of a body meant there was nothing to alert me to the fact that what I was doing might be wrong. And since there was little risk of that body ever being closer than thousands of miles away from mine, I typed on.

I am not sure what it was that made me carry on this exchange—to correspond with someone I didn't know. I don't think it was loneliness that made me tap back funny stories to Jonathan when I should have been working. Maybe it was that I was, as my husband would later come to say about me, selfish. I really did not think of what I was doing as disloyal, though looking back, there was something unmistakably ajar in our marriage. To me, it seemed as though my husband was not interested in the things that I did or thought anyway. We rarely did anything together other than preach or go to meetings. We had filled up the emotional gap between us with our ministry, our language learning, our saving of people's lives. Beyond our shared belief system, there wasn't much that we had in common. He certainly didn't want to talk about podcasts.

And maybe I *was* selfish. Any activity other than using your life in service to the organization and God's kingdom was considered selfishness. Among my people, the brotherhood of Jehovah's Witnesses, there were those whose ancestors had been in concentration camps for their faith—in fact, Witnesses were the only ones who were allowed out of Hitler's concentration camps if they renounced their faith. And they didn't. In China, a Jehovah's Witness missionary had been imprisoned in solitary confinement for years in the 1950s, for preaching after Mao came to power. Kids with cancer chose death rather than take a blood transfusion. My culture was one of biblical proportions: men sacrificing their own children at God's request, fathers who allowed angry crowds to rape their daughters to protect God's angels. So to sit at a desk and type sentences to a worldly man was an abhorrent selfishness.

Still, it was just a conversation, and having a conversation was not wrong, even in our strict set of beliefs. If I noticed my heart would lift along with the three-note scale that sounded with the pop-up on my screen each morning around 10:00 a.m., I ignored it, like I had ignored my heart for years. A religious person learns to live with a divided heart, one that does not acknowledge what it does not want to admit to itself.

What I had started to notice, however, was that it was exciting to share these everyday things with someone. I was living a life so separate and secreted from people, because of the nature of the preaching we did, and there was so much to share. And while I could not share the preaching part with him, he was interested in what it was like here, what I did, and what I thought about. He paid attention to my ideas, he thought I was smart and had things to offer the world. I was surprised that someone would think of me in this way, since it was so far from how I thought about myself. I had been primed as a child to evade notice. I had been taught by my faith that to stand out from the crowd was to be lacking in humility, that displaying any kind of intellect was prideful, and that to pursue one's interests or talents was wrong, especially as a woman. The beloved woman was one who went about her preaching and household work with diligence, letting her husband do the speaking. I never did that well, but I tried.

This ongoing conversation soon became habit forming, and after a couple of months, when I would arrive at work and get online each morning, Jonathan would be there waiting for me. We started coming up with ideas together, and just for fun he began helping me with the writing assignments I had. He was very intelligent, and the lesson introductions he wrote were full of razor-sharp wit. It was strange to talk to someone this often and not know what they looked like, so one day he let down his wall of privacy and sent me a picture of himself, from college. He was very tall, with dark hair, and intense brown eyes. He wasn't quite as I had pictured him, but close. Of course he knew what I looked like already, from the pictures on the website.

Though I now had a mental picture of him as we corresponded, Jonathan would still answer almost none of my questions about himself in a satisfying way. If I asked about his writing, he would say that he couldn't discuss it, because it involved a Hollywood film with a big star. If I asked about his family or friends, or what he did in his free time, he would give one-word answers. I had given up on trying until a day when our conversations veered from their usual topics. To my surprise, given all the subjects he would avoid, when spirituality snuck into my conversation despite myself, Jonathan seemed very interested, and he began to share how he looked at life. I was excited to find an "in," to find some way to know more about him, to correct the lopsidedness of our conversation. For me, spirituality equaled my religion, thus it was inevitable that one day it would come up. In code, of course.

It did not go well.

I had laid down hints for weeks about the things I believed, excited that I had finally found a topic on which he would share things about himself, but also alarmed, because every viewpoint he had was so contrary to my own Witness worldview. The more he talked the more he diverged into territory that sounded utterly Satanic to me. I would drop little hints about what I thought, trying to find some common ground somewhere. But there was no overlap between the two.

Finally he asked me which religion I believed in, and I panicked at having the question even show up on my Gchat. I was terrified of the Chinese authorities, which we knew monitored people's communications, seeing it and targeting me. I tried to walk it back a bit, and then told him using a code—"Think of who the person is that testifies in a court case." That was all it took and he knew.

When I came out with it, he said, "I knew it. I knew you were under the control of something."

I was taken aback. And mad. But he was forceful and didn't care about tact. He was so sure of himself that I didn't even know how to counter it. I was just as forceful: I believed in it so fully and practiced it so intensely, there was no way that I was under something's control. I was an intelligent creation of God with my own mind, I knew this, and my beliefs were between me and God, and none of his business, I insisted.

Jonathan: But are they your beliefs?

Me: Of course they are. I believe they are the truth.

Jonathan: Where did they come from?

Me: The Bible.

Jonathan: Okay, but why do you need that organization then?

Me: Because they give us spiritual food, from the Bible.

Jonathan: Why can't you just read the book yourself? Why do they know any more than you do?

Me: God's always had an organization.

Jonathan: Has he? Who? When?

Me: Yes.

Jonathan: Is that what they told you?

And thus, we arrived at the arguing phase of our relationship, having still never met in person. Yet we were sufficiently intimate by this point to spar over religion, on Gchat, in code, so as not to alert the Chinese Internet eavesdroppers ("bble" for Bible, "jz" for Jesus, "big A" for Armageddon).

I had spent almost all of my free time for my entire adult life talking about my religion, but rarely had I ever listened to anyone on the same topic. When someone we preached to at the doors tried to give us literature of their own, or anti–Jehovah's Witness literature for that matter (of which there was some circulating in the world), we would have a comeback all ready at hand: come find me at *my* door and I will listen to *you*. But encountering these words on a screen disarmed me. Had they been said to me in person, I would have blocked them out, as I always had when I heard things critical of my faith. Staring at them here, I was pulled in.

The more I argued with him, the more direct Jonathan became. At first I thought of this as a chance to preach to him, to teach him the truth, but the more I found myself unable to counter his arguments, the more I knew that it was Satan behind his attacks on my faith. We studied all the time about how Satan knew our weaknesses, that he would come into my Gchat in a friend's clothing like this and that it was my fault for ignoring all the warnings. Regardless, I engaged. I kept thinking, much like my grandmother, that I would prove him wrong.

But there was a problem. The more he pointed out that the things I said were just programming, and the more I argued that they weren't, I would find that his words would stick in my head. When he went to bed in his time zone, and I was awake in mine, his questions would linger in the back of my mind and fester. I would first rage against him: he was blind and arrogant and dismissed what was dear to me in ways no one ever had before. He was clearly from Satan and blinded by him, and didn't have any better answers than I did. And while, yes, he was right about some things—the Governing Body did tell us over and over again not to read anything either on the Internet or in print that was from "apostates"—that kind of control was for our own safety. He was the perfect example of this. Satan used those things to try and destroy our faith. I knew this. Yet here I was, revealing these bits of myself that he would tear up as if they were my pamphlets, right before my eyes.

And it wasn't like Jonathan was some kind of an expert on my religion. He had only done what I had not dared to: read about Jehovah's Witnesses on the Internet. He watched videos made by people who had left. He read articles. Soon he was telling me what I believed, rather than the reverse.

Then he began to tell me how these organizations control not only their members' behavior but also their information intake, thoughts, and even emotions. I scoffed at the idea that I was controlled. But when Jonathan asked me if I could be friends with people I chose, or whether they dictated what clothes or hairstyles we could wear, I couldn't deny that those things were true.

Jonathan: What about food?

Me: No one tells me what to eat, what are you talking about? Okay we don't eat anything with blood in it, which I mean that is gross anyway. Or take a blood transfusion, which actually protects us.

Jonathan: I saw that. So you are cool with dying then.

Me: No, JW have pioneered the field of bloodless surgery. It's better for you than taking blood.

Jonathan: But people die, there's all kinds of Witnesses who have died who didn't have to. God needs you to do that?

Witnesses chalked up the cases in the media about Witnesses dying after refusing blood transfusions to doctors' errors most of the time, or as no great consequence, because the person would be resurrected. The most important thing was not to preserve your life, because then you would die at Armageddon anyway; the most important thing was to stay faithful. There was an entire *Awake!* magazine that showed all the children and teenagers who had died faithful for not taking blood, holding them up as examples of faith.

Jonathan: What about time for yourself? What about having to
report the amount of time you preach? What about all your
rigid rules?

I stopped him there. I could not tolerate any more.

I worked half distractedly, countering his arguments in my
head while he slept, and by morning again my anger would
have ebbed, I would have put the thoughts aside and would be
looking forward to the moment that I saw "Taipan is online"
flip to the bottom right of my computer screen. Our passion on
opposite stances of this argument became one more string that
entangled us.

Parallel to these more charged interchanges, our other conversations went on, too. And in these conversations, I was the
Amber of ChinesePod, the Amber who no one knew was hiding the secret of her religion and who everyone thought
was a normal person. And in that sphere, Jonathan and I did
not argue. We collaborated. After Jonathan heard me on the
"Qing Wen" podcast that day I filled in, he pinged me.

Jonathan: I have an idea.

He said it was time for a new show at ChinesePod, and he
had come up with a concept for me, one that he was sure would
be a huge hit, and that would make me a "star." I laughed a
little about this Hollywood sheen on our back-alley podcasts,
but I put that day's argument to bed early and listened, in-
trigued.

When I heard Jonathan's idea, I loved it. And while I knew that he was right, that it was a great idea, I had no confidence that I could pull it off. I also knew that it was not possible for me to seek these kinds of ambitious things for myself. For one thing, I was a Witness, and all the Witnesses would find out that I was doing this, pursuing this career, because everything I did would be on the Internet, for all to see. I didn't dare tell Jonathan this reason, though, so as not to give him any more ammunition. But beyond that, there was the issue of notoriety. If I did work that had a public face, using my real name, wouldn't there be a risk that I would be recognized by someone, at some point? I was supposed to be undercover.

And finally, though I felt superior in a religious sense to the people around me, I felt insecure about my abilities at work. I had no college degree, which to some may not seem to be a prerequisite for doing a podcast, but to me felt like a blot that marked me as inferior and unqualified. I did not know what I hadn't learned. I tried to hide my fears of this, but deep down I worried that I could not succeed in the way people who understood the world better than I did could.

"Stop putting up your resistance," he would say. "That's your indoctrination speaking." My blood would boil.

But, of course, the idea excited me. And while having a career had been something unthinkable in my life as a Witness, I really liked this work, I liked being part of life, engaging with it and with people, and I couldn't help but want to create, to be part of things. This was another portion of myself to hide on the days I was not at work, and which I had hidden from even myself for my entire life. And now the Internet had opened a door for me to realize these things about myself, to exist in the world in some half-real fashion. And though I had very little faith in myself, Jonathan's complete certainty that I was just the person to do it carried me forward.

I decided to give it a try. I put my fears and reservations aside because deep down, I was very excited about the idea. I came up with a pitch for my bosses, who barely knew my name. I was the person who came in three days a week and didn't talk much, and didn't hang around with them after work. I recorded a pilot on my lunch breaks and after work, and had it ready when I sent the proposal for my show:

DEAR AMBER—SHOW PROPOSAL
ChinesePod's Insider Guide to Everything China

VISION:

Dear Amber is ChinesePod's Insider's all-access guide to Everything China. It is a witty, insightful, and entertaining show that answers questions about China that people have wondered about but have never had anyone to ask.

SHOW FORMAT/STRUCTURE:

In the vein of the 50-year hit "Dear Abby," which is read by more people than any other newspaper column worldwide, Dear Amber will be structured as an "advice columnist" show, with answers to everyday questions about culture, learning Chinese, food, travel, relationships, slang, and more.

The answer given for each question will be well researched and insightful, specifically from the standpoint of experience gained from living in China and studying Chinese with ChinesePod. Certain questions will be answered in collaboration with a Chinese or foreign guest or cohost. Anecdotes and stories from real life will add entertainment value.

SAMPLE DEAR AMBER SHOW CONTENT:

Italiana writes: "Dear Amber, I'm very interested in trying out my new Mandarin skills by watching Chinese television. Do you have any shows you would recommend that I might be able to understand?"

Well, Italiana, there's nothing like a good Chinese soap opera, where the Taitai accuses the husband of having an affair with an acrobat from the Chinese opera troupe, and the nosy neighbors are suspicious that the grandma cooked

their missing pet chicken for Chinese New Year cele-
bration. Not to mention that you get to see the occasional
token foreigner trying out his poor acting skills, which is
always good for a laugh. To start with, though, I think
soaps may be a little advanced, with obscure dialogue and
heavy Taiwanese accents.

So before you graduate to this kind of melodrama, I
suggest you start with children's shows. When I started
learning Chinese, the kids' shows were not only educational but FUN TO WATCH! My current favorite is
"_____," it's about . . .

Taipan asks: **"Dear Amber, I am thinking of coming to
China, but when I looked up tickets on the usual websites
the prices were astronomical. What's with that? I thought
it was supposed to be pretty cheap to fly from LA to
Shanghai."**

Ah, Taipan, your question brings up some fond and some
not-so-fond memories of my first trips over the Pacific.
The good news is there are tons of options. The travel
website prices fluctuate greatly, so sometimes you can find
a decently priced ticket.

One factor to consider is peak travel times. At Chinese
New Year and during summer vacation there are, no exaggeration, millions of Chinese nationals crisscrossing the
skies to get back to visit family and attend luck-inspiring
banquets. Prices skyrocket during those periods.

As far as getting the best deal on a ticket the rest of the

time—those of us living here know the Chinese know how to wrangle a good deal, so your best bet would be to plan an afternoon outing to your local Chinatown. No matter what city you live in, there should be one in some form, and Chinese travel agents often specialize in tours and flights to Asia—they buy in bulk, and if you use your Mandarin, they just might give you better deals on seats.

Not only will you likely pay less, but you will also get your first taste of how business goes down here. In my case, it was Winnie who gave me my education. She was from Hong Kong. When I walked off the pungent streets of Chinatown Vancouver into her dark, eight-foot-by-eight-foot agency wallpapered with aging, water-stained travel posters, I was greeted by a hand waving me over to a chair. I knew I was in the right place. Winnie gave me a deal. She never forgot me either. Once a year I would return to the strange comfort that, though everything else seemed to be changing in the city after I had gone, Wankow Travel never changed. Not even that stack of travel brochures from 1982.

The bosses listened to my pilot and agreed to let me do the show.

t turned out, to my surprise, that being a podcast host came naturally to me. I now had an outlet for my curiosity. I liked interviewing people. All those years of prying into people's lives, drawing them out so as to convert them, was a skill I could use in the real world. And I knew so much about China, compared to a lot of foreigners here, because I had been so intimate with my Bible students, dating back over years, to when I had first started preaching to people from China in my hometown. Also, if I didn't know the answer to something, I had Chinese Bible students and friends whom I could ask.

Even more surprising, though, was that Jonathan was right: the show quickly became very popular. After the pilot was approved, I began to make one weekly show that came out on Saturday mornings. Before the questions began rolling in from the listeners, I wrote the first few questions myself, because I knew from experience which questions people would have when they were new to Chinese culture. Within weeks, iTunes had chosen it from thousands of podcasts to feature in its newsletter and on its home page. The audience got very big, very fast, after that. Kind of bigger than I could comprehend. Later, iTunes ranked it as one of the top ten podcasts of the year.

People soon were writing from around the world, asking questions for the show:

Amber: This question comes from Steve. "Dear Amber, Why do so many people outside in China wear surgical masks?"

Thanks for your question, Steve. You are not alone in wondering about this. Clay's asked this question himself, and he's here to answer it, together with me.

Clay: Yes, I am very baffled by this practice!

Amber: Now the weather has turned cold here in China, and yes, there is a plethora of surgical masks—well, it's not limited to surgical masks, there are also a lot of Winnie-the-Poohs, made of fabric. There are homemade masks, Hello Kitty masks.

Clay: You see them a lot.

Amber: I think our first reaction when we do see this is like, "Ew, oh, disease, stay away. TB or something." But after talking to some locals, I realized that this is generally not the reason people are wearing it. And those who seem like they have TB are probably not wearing one is my guess.

Clay: But even if they did, I mean, the masks are often homemade.

Amber: True. But the first reason has to do with the Chinese trepidation about wind. Wind is considered the major cause of illness in traditional Chinese medicine. It combines easily with other pathogens, and so wind in the face can be a dire thing, leading to syndromes known as wind cold, wind heat, and wind dampness. So, often, people wear a mask so the wind will not blow into their face.

Clay: It will kill you.

Amber: I also fear cold, so I don't blame them.

Clay: No, you don't fear cold. You told me you often walk outside with wet hair, and your neighbors scold you.

Amber: Oh, that's true. I guess I fear it in different ways. I fear cold feet in bed.

Clay: Ha-ha.

Amber: Myself, I think a scarf is more comfortable, and I can say this firsthand because I, too, have worn a surgical mask, personally, so I know about the subject. But that being said, first we're going to teach you how to say "wear a mask" in Chinese: *dai kouzhao*. That literally means "put on mouth cover."

Clay: Wait, let's back up for a minute here. When did you ever wear one of these?

Amber: Well, I am an expert of sorts on this topic, sort of, because I was in Taiwan during the peak of the SARS epidemic, a few years ago. *And* not that I was a paranoid freak or thought that the mask would protect me—okay, maybe I am—but at that time, the peak of SARS, if you wanted to take the subway, and I was going to Chinese school every day, so I had to, it was a requirement that you wear that mask.

Clay: Was it really, the government required it?

Amber: Yes, they wouldn't let you in the subway other-
wise. But you know, I think it was more a mental peace
sort of thing, because people were, like, touching them
all the time, adjusting them. I mean, someone took the
mask off to cough, I saw that happen. And some of
them were, as I said, Winnie-the-Pooh masks, they're
not really stopping any germs.

Clay: So was yours, like, a doctor-approved kind of mask,
or like some kind of thing concocted with a sock,
or . . . ?

Amber: It was. My roommate came home with a box of
surgical masks, I'm not sure where she got them, I
think she had a friend who was a dentist's assistant or
from the night market or something. It was pretty hot
and humid that time of year, and I can tell you that
there is nothing worse than your hot-air breath blow-
ing out into a hot, humid, sweaty surgical face mask. It
was awful.

Clay: So, any other reason why more in winter?

Amber: Just to keep their face warm, basically. That's another reason.

Clay: Kind of like a windshield.

Amber: Yeah!

Clay: An ugly windshield.

Amber: But it works, you hook it around your ears, it's
convenient. It's reusable. Connie also said that in the
northern parts of China there are a lot of sandstorms,
so it actually does help to have this thing on your face.

Clay: We use bandannas for that in Texas. Kidding.

Amber: (laughs) Oh, like a cowboy. Another thing, though, the practice wasn't as prevalent before SARS, but people have become a lot more conscious of germs. So they will even wear them now to avoid infecting other people when they are sick with a cold or something.

Clay: Hmm, I don't know if the Winnie-the-Pooh is really going to save us. . . .

Amber: It's the thought that counts.

Clay: Yes.

Amber: I mean, there are so many people crowded into the subway, if nothing else it might give you a sense of security. But you can just put on your bandanna, Clay.

Now, I also know of another big reason why people wore the masks in Taiwan: to keep out the pollution, especially when they were riding their motorbikes. However, I read an article that debunked that idea; apparently, pollution particles are too small for any surgical mask to be able to block them. Too bad. But at least it keeps the dirt off your face, anyway. We're used to it now, but I do remember feeling nervous the first time I saw one here.

Clay: Yeah, the only person I've ever seen wear one before this is a doctor, or a guy mowing his lawn.

Amber: It's like a universal tool, it can be used to keep out wind, sand, germs—at least in your own mind.

Clay: Lawn clippings.

Amber: Are there any lawns here, Clay, speaking of? I've never seen one.

Listeners visited Shanghai and were starstruck when they came to the office to meet us. I went from complete self-induced invisibility to this person—this persona—and it felt surreal. I would tell Jonathan all about it, about the gifts they brought, about the stories they told me that I had told them, about how well they seemed to know me, from listening to me talk about life here. I couldn't even tell a story without them saying, "Oh yes, like that time you . . ." Someone sent me my favorite band's album. Others mailed me coffee when I said on air that it was hard to get in China. After each episode, Jonathan and I talked about the things that were on the show that day.

One morning Jonathan brought up a book that he had found online. It was written by a member of the Governing Body of the Witnesses who left the religion in the 1980s. My body filled with electric fear. I had heard of this book, once. It was the apostate book of apostate books, and the man who wrote it, we were told, had become prideful and wanted worship for himself, like Satan. And that was why he had left the organization and written this book.

Jonathan was reading the book, which is about five hundred pages long. He started to ask me questions that normal worldly people don't ask. "Did you know this thing about the org being part of the UN?"

"That's ridiculous, the UN is part of the wild beast of Revelation, and it's a tool of Satan," I said. What was he talking about? How did he even know this?

"This dude seems pretty smart and normal," Jonathan told me, about the ex-Witness who wrote this book. "And they kicked him out when he was, like, eighty or something!"

I was afraid of the book. To me the book seemed as if it were an alive thing, that its pages would creep out of the cover and slice me up, then throw me out onto the street, worldly and alone. The book would manipulate me, it had a secret power to dislodge truth. This was what we had always been told. That the truth could be stolen from us.

My husband was not interested in my podcast, except to warn me that as a result of the show I was becoming too involved with the world. He never even listened to it. I knew that if we were back home, the elders would talk to me, to shepherd me and counsel me. But in China, the few elders who were here were at far-flung corners of an enormous city, and we saw each other only once a week. Everyone had their own lives in between and no one seemed to pay much attention to what anyone was doing on the Internet.

Meanwhile, the tension in me was building. The city had turned from frigid to hot almost overnight, and I was suddenly, feverishly, looking at everything around me, from the meal in front of me, to the man I lived with, to the materials I read in preparation for the Sunday meetings, and asking "Why?" I was in a constant distracted state of questioning. I was questioning with a mind that had been trained not to. It was highly uncomfortable.

One day I rode my bike to an appointment in a different part of town. I parked my bike and locked it to a pole with its thick, long chain, as had now become my practice, after my first bike was stolen. As I walked away, a middle-aged woman came out of her doorway and began yelling at me. She motioned to my bike, complaining that it was blocking her entrance. I looked back. My bike was about seven feet from her doorway, which in China equals what one might think of as ten car lengths in North America. No one ever complained about this. In fact, I noticed that there were bikes parked along the curb next to mine, even closer to her doorway.

"*Laowai* (foreigner), move this bicycle!" she yelled at me.

"Why?" I said.

"You are in my way."

"But all these bikes are parked here. I am not near your door."

"This is my property."

A crowd began to form. I had watched aghast at street fights like this when I first arrived; now I had lived here long enough to become the one in the middle of the fighting ring. I couldn't help but be a little surprised and impressed that my Chinese had progressed to the point that I could use it to argue. I didn't know what to do, and for some reason it felt impossible to disengage from this discussion, mostly because that would involve me losing face (a Chinese cultural concept that one can't help but be affected by after many years of living with it) by unlocking my bike and moving it to another location, in front of this audience of potential hecklers. A foreigner arguing with a Shanghainese woman was too much entertainment to resist. But I could hear murmurs in the crowd, and it seemed like at least some people saw my point. I saw one person motion toward the woman's door and then my bike, then back again to the door, a gesture I took as one of solidarity. Jesus would have turned the other cheek, but I didn't.

I was still standing near my bike, and the woman was now yelling at someone in the crowd who was picking up the argument I didn't have the language skills to win. They were yelling at each other now.

A policeman was at the corner, and it occurred to me that maybe the best answer was to ask the policeman to settle the matter of whether my bike should be moved. If he acquitted me, perhaps we could all return to our corners of the street and our business, all "faces" intact. If he indicted me, well, then I could skulk away to my bike and hopeful obscurity around the bend in the road (though somehow, with the way I stood out, I imagined people coming up to me, years from now, saying, "Aren't you the woman who . . .").

I walked to the end of the block, and a few from the crowd, my posse of sorts, followed me. The policeman noticed and watched our approach with a calm eye. I greeted him and explained to him the situation the best that I could. He said that he would come over as soon as he finished writing a ticket. I waited, and he walked back to the scene of the crime with me.

I held forth, the crowd quieted.

"Officer, can you tell me, in the People's Republic of China, is a sidewalk considered public property?"

"Yes, it is," he said. Some in the crowd nodded their agreement.

"In China, is there any law against parking one's bike on the sidewalk, as I have here?"

"No, there is not," he said.

The woman motioned angrily at the police officer, and began speaking to him in Shanghainese, a language I could not understand. I didn't know what she said, but she was clearly upset, pointing at her door, pointing at my bike.

The officer remained calm, escorted her to her doorway to have a look, then returned. I asked the policeman whether I had to move my bike. He said that I did not. The crowd let out a rumble. The Shanghainese woman stormed back toward her door, complaining to a neighbor and pointing at me, shouting. The cop told me that he was a traffic cop and had to return to the corner, but if we wanted to go to court over the matter, we could.

I was now late for my appointment and shaking a little with the adrenaline of the whole matter. The crowd was dispersing; the woman stood glowering at me from her doorway. I put my bag over my shoulder and tried to slink away as unobtrusively as possible.

"BANG!"

I turned around. The woman had pushed my bike over, onto the street, still attached to the pole with its thick chain. It lay there with one wheel spinning slowly, wretchedly.

I looked down at it for a moment, and back at the doorway. The woman had returned to her house, the two pieces of red fabric that often hung over the doors of Chinese homes flapping a little in the wind. The shiny red pillars of her doorway looked like those on old Chinese temples. I realized that I was defeated. I was on her turf, no matter how long I might have lived here, or how much this felt like home. I walked back to my bike, lifted it upright, unlocked it, and pushed it across the street and around the corner to another pole I found, and locked it there.

Jonathan, or as he was programmed into my phone, Tai-pan, texted me before I had a chance to tell my husband the story. I had begun to feel guilty, now that our interactions had expanded outside the walls of my workplace, but I couldn't help but write him back to tell him about what had happened. Talking to him was now the most natural thing in my world. He knew more about me than my husband, in a way. Or, at least, it felt like he saw more of who I was.

WE FOUND ANOTHER overlapping awake hour, late in the evening Shanghai time, when my husband was out at a Bible study or was busy writing talks for the sermons he would deliver on Sunday at the secret meetings. Neither Jonathan nor I wanted to think of ourselves as people who would have an affair, so we stuck to topics of spirituality so that we could assure ourselves that we were not doing anything wrong.

> Me: Unless I have something that can make me feel as sure as I do now about what I believe, I wouldn't be able to walk away from it. . . .

> Jonathan: I don't expect you to. Keep it. I've tried to be the source of unlocking your death grip, but you can free your mind by doing the work, so that you can relax your grip on your own.

> In AA, some people say that a person cannot really change until they hit rock bottom. You haven't hit rock bottom yet.

Me: But if I free my mind, I lose the sure hope that I believe I have. That this isn't the real life, that what my life is like now is not the most important thing. How can I just forget that? It's so hard to imagine it not being true, when I look at the state of the world.

Jonathan: When I look at the state of the world . . . those are canned answers/phrases.

Imagine that something else is possible. Pry your mind open with whatever tools you have left that haven't been indoctrinated into the cult.

Me: Pry it open to what?

Jonathan: Give up your previous notions you may have about god and life.

Why are you so afraid to open your mind to other thoughts?

What do you fear?

Being wrong?

Being ostracized?

Me: Not at all.

Jonathan: Being a sinner? What then?

Me: I just need something concrete.

Something real.

Jonathan: So you fear uncertainty.

You fear that if 1% of the Bible is untrue then your life has no meaning.

Which is an illusion that you've created for yourself that is intensified by the fact that you preach, so the stakes are higher.

Me: It's not like that. I learn together with my Bible students.

Jonathan: Preach teach share reach.

Whatever.

You speak and people fucking listen.

Me: It's not like that.

Jonathan: If it's as a student then you have a leader because it's not a student mind-set that you approach it with. It's a rote mind-set.

The fact is that throughout history god has given us messengers in all cultures and times and walks of life, Jesus being one of them, you being another.

Do you believe god favors men over women?

Me: Not at all.

Jonathan: Yet the Bible and all the prophets in it are men. Do you think god favors whites to non-whites?

Me: No, I don't. Not at all, the white/non-white thing that's a human problem.

Jonathan: Why didn't god give his one true book to Chinese or Africans?

So women are equal to men in the Bible? God could have started it anywhere and he chose Whiteville.

Me: It says right in the Bible that god views every race of person acceptable to him.

Jonathan: But clearly he favors men. . . .

Oh well . . . I wish all the Asians, black people, Latinos, and women luck with their salvation.

Me: Being a male prophet doesn't mean you have some special salvation.

Jonathan: And does god really expect us to believe Noah's Ark? And why aren't dinosaurs mentioned?

Me: You know, scientifically, there is a theory that is compatible with a flood theory. You can't really say for sure if it's not true or is true, because you weren't there, right?

Jonathan: lol

Me: I don't know. What?

Jonathan: I can laugh out loud at the thought of applying logic to everything else except when applying logic doesn't serve me.

Me: Oh right. Ha-ha. Don't worry, I hear what you're saying, I do.

Jonathan: And if you think the Bible has logic, then you have to suspend your logic to believe the Noah's Ark story. And what about fucking dinosaurs?!

WTF? And dinosaur heads seem really fucking real too.

Show me the book on brontosaurus.

Me: Well, it doesn't mention a lot of things. It's not a zoology or botany or whatever book.

Jonathan: Don't you think for a second that if the Bible were LITERALLY true, literally our history, that someone would have mentioned the giant fucking lizard?

But more important—if it had been meant for today, don't you think it would address ANY of the things that we face today?

Me: But it does address tons of stuff we face today.

Jonathan: But not most:

Man's relationship with his environment

Talking with strange men over the Internet

;)

He had a point.

I felt close to Jonathan while simultaneously knowing I should run the other way. He represented the end of everything that made me feel safe, everything that gave me peace of mind, everything that made my life what it was. But I wanted to keep talking to him. Contradiction is more easily endured when it is pleasurable. The incongruity that had begun to emerge in the rest of my life, on the other hand, was less easily borne.

Months passed like this, in a holding pattern. I went to meetings. I went on my Bible studies, I tried to preach, I did what I had always done, but I felt like a hypocrite. I had doubts. But if I didn't believe, my life would be over, and everything would be gone. I was paralyzed, because there was no answer to this problem. The stakes were too high to do anything.

I sat at the meetings and followed along in the *Watchtower* study, but I could not control my mind anymore. I questioned: Who wrote this? How do I know that they are right? And then, sometimes, I began to feel irritated when they would say the man is head of the woman. This rule seemed to get harped on disproportionately. Why were we following rules from a society that no longer existed, that didn't work anymore?

Still, in one regard, I hadn't changed at all since I was eight, and my reason for staying in it was the same, more than twenty years later: fear.

I have never been good at keeping my mouth shut and pretending. One night I was sitting at home, reading one of our publications to prepare for the meeting, as I had done my whole life. My husband was in the chair across the room. My eye moved down the page to an article that was to be discussed at the next meeting. Its topic was "Food at the Proper Time."

Reading the headline, I already knew what might be coming.

Does "the faithful and discreet slave" endorse independent groups of Witnesses who meet together to engage in Scriptural research or debate? —Matt. 24:45, 47

The scripture that the headline was taken from was the one that the Governing Body (which also calls itself "the faithful and discreet slave") constantly cites as the evidence that they and only they were qualified to interpret the Bible and give us our spiritual instruction. And that anything from any other source, or any independent thought, was dangerous or bad.

I read on. The article said that some brothers and sisters had been forming their own study groups, and learning Hebrew or Greek so that they could read the Bible in its original language. Others had formed groups to explore scientific subjects related to the Bible.

What a great idea, I thought to myself.

I kept going. The article noted that these practices should be immediately stopped, because our spiritual food was to come through the Governing Body, and only them, as they were God's mouthpiece and had been tasked with looking after our spiritual needs. Any who wished to do extra Bible study or research should do so using only the publications written and published by the Governing Body.

In the past, I would have read this, numb, unthinking, obedient. But I read this now and blurted out, "Is this some kind of a fucking cult or something?"

Why did God give us a brain, if we were not supposed to use it to think, or learn, or seek to understand?

There was a long pause, then my husband said, "What . . . did you just say?"

A Witness cannot just fade away without anyone trying to intervene, and it was hard to find enough mental space to gain any perspective. It's not the kind of religion that lets you walk away, because the people in it think that by walking away, you have lost your mind and interventions will bring you to your senses. Who would give up on everlasting life, on the truth? It would be one thing if I was on my own, or single—then I could perhaps just disappear. But here I was, married to an elder, a pioneer missionary. All my friends were Witnesses. Almost all of my family were Witnesses. And I myself was still on the books as a pioneer missionary, too. When someone like me no longer believed, they were considered a traitor—God's enemy, an apostate.

I knew this well, I had read this in our literature my entire life. Apostates are "mentally diseased," "depraved," a "dog that has returned to its own vomit," and "lower than a snake" in the books that we studied, in the talks that we listened to, week in and week out. There were entire articles we studied at our meetings and hour-long sermons that warned of people like me:

Satan was the first creature to turn apostate. Modern-day apostates display characteristics similar to those of the

Devil. Their mind may be poisoned by a critical attitude toward individuals in the congregations, Christian elders, or the Governing Body. Like their father, Satan, apostates target people of integrity. (John 8:44) No wonder servants of Jehovah avoid all contact with them!

Like gangrene, apostate reasoning is nothing but quick-spreading spiritual death. If the one spreading apostate teachings cannot be restored to spiritual health . . . amputation of this member (disfellowshipping) may be the only alternative.

Apostates are "mentally diseased," and they seek to infect others with their disloyal teachings. They "quietly" bring their ideas into the congregation, like criminals who secretly bring things into a country.

Interesting point, that last one, remembering the literature we had been told to smuggle in our suitcases when we came to China.

I looked across at my husband and wondered how to reconcile all of these things. I had yet to see an article that told a man what to do when his wife is an apostate; how it was possible to both not welcome her in their home and not be permitted to divorce her.

All of these things made me feel like I was going crazy. I was trapped. And so was he. I began to wonder how much longer I could keep this up.

Still, come Sunday, I put on my dress and left the house and went to the meeting, because that was what I had always done.

Shortly after this, my husband went away on a trip home and did not contact me for the entire two weeks. With him so absent, the floodgates opened. Jonathan and I talked all day, and then all night, too. I didn't imagine doing anything wrong with him, I just imagined being away from all of this. Being in a place where I could forget about Armageddon for a while, with someone who understood, where no one knew me.

Me: I like to picture nice things we could do together in LA. But I don't know if it will ever happen.

Jonathan: Of course it will. Why would you say that?

Me: I don't know.

Jonathan: Are you depressed right now?

Me: Because I'm immersed in this world I guess. No, not depressed.

Jonathan: Good.

Me: I just don't know if I can change my whole way of life. . . . I am wondering if I will be haunted.

Jonathan: You will get through it, I promise.

Stop jumping to fatalism. You're in a cult, it takes time to shed the programming you've received.

Me: I'm not 100% sure it's a bad cult though.

Jonathan: Amber, it's a cult.

Me: But, here is the thing.

Jonathan: Don't worry about it right now, you've got enough on your plate. Here's the thing:

You're in a cult, and you've replaced yourself with someone else's programming.

Me: I don't think I can ever be like other people.

Jonathan: Yes, you can. Stop projecting and be at peace with dealing day to day, instead of giving up on the now for the future.

Me: I'm not going off the deep end, I'm just thinking long and hard about it.

Because it's a big deal, when someone accuses what you have built your life around of being a cult.

Jonathan: It's a big deal, I totally agree.

Me: I find it impossible to believe that some parts of it aren't true, so it's hard to say I can completely walk away from it.

Jonathan: There is no questioning that even taking a few steps away from where you've been confined for so long will feel like your world has been yanked out from under you.

But this is a day-to-day thing—you can't just suddenly stop being a JW, because its tentacles reach into every part of your life.

Me: I know.

Jonathan: And you'll learn to stop thinking like one and deprogramming the fear that has been stamped into you. You can look for answers without the guidance of a dozen men back east.

Freedom is a frightening thing, that's why so many people go back to jail after they've been released, because they can't face life without everything controlled for them. It happens all the time.

We as humans seem to work the hardest to avoid our biggest gift—freedom of choice.

We want to be told what to think, what to do, how to talk, what to believe, how to believe, how to help, how to rote.

You know the Watchtower is wrong about some things, and therefore it can be wrong about other things which you are not aware of yet. You can be godly and good and pure without them.

Me: Can I ask you something though?

Jonathan: no

seriously, no

Me: ha-ha

Why?

Jonathan: Because it's a loaded question.

Me: You took the dog from the side of the road.

You like to take care of/save things/people don't you?

Do you feel like you have to rescue me or something?

Jonathan: I like you, so I'm willing to try. If I stop liking you, my willpower will shrink.

Me: What does that mean—because you like me, you have the desire to get into all this?

Jonathan: yes

Me: funny

Jonathan: Why?

Me: Because "this" is such a big part of me, but that's the part you think I should get rid of.

Jonathan: I dig you, I'm doing god's service ;)

I'm like Jodie Foster in Silence of the Lambs.

Me: Does that make me Anthony Hopkins?

Jonathan: Rescuing this one lamb's free will from the slaughter.

He called my phone on the weekend, and I heard his voice for the first time, which made me terribly nervous, because behind this voice was a real person. The alternate, abstract Internet world I'd been inhabiting within this already unrecognizable place my life had become was worming its way into my real life.

When my husband returned from his trip, I asked him if he loved me. I thought I knew what the answer would be, but I felt that he needed to hear himself say it. We had been coexisting for almost a decade, in a relationship that should have been a college romance but was now a lifelong sentence. Years of enforced togetherness, of secret regrets, of suffocating apathy had now become unbearable to the point that even something hurtful would feel better than this feeling of nothing. It wasn't like we hated each other, we were just loveless. Lovelessness was worse than loneliness; it sucked the life out of everything we did. It was a leaden cloak suffocating warm flesh. I was exhausted from dragging the relationship around the world in an attempt to revive it. He had given up on me long ago. I don't know that he had ever even really known how to try.

He replied that he didn't think he loved me. He sometimes thought he needed to be with a dumb girl, he said. It almost gave me a thrill, to know what he really thought, even if it hurt.

This admission was at least some kind of intimacy, the kind not normally between us.

That night I drank an entire bottle of wine. I had to find a way out. The two of us in this house were like animals in a zoo; we were here because of a piece of paper we had signed when we were just barely adults. We were here because the Bible said we had to live together. We were here in this cage so the elders could walk by and make sure we were keeping our vows, so that others with bad marriages didn't see an unlocked door and follow us out. But I could not help but wonder: Why did God need us to stay together? Weren't there bigger problems to worry about?

My husband watched me drink and begged me, not to save our marriage, but to save myself. He wanted me to go to the elders so they could help me back from the brink of apostasy, this death sentence. I cried, drunk, and told him I couldn't do this anymore. He thought I was having some kind of breakdown, but I was not. I was trying to telegraph to him that he needed to leave me. I was telling him I could not live this life anymore and thought that maybe if I screamed it he would understand the danger he was in. That he would run out the door and be protected from the fiery apocalypse that was coming to our home, because though I knew not how it would come, I knew that the day and the hour were near.

But he did not leave, he would wait for the paradise, he said, when all would be made right. It was the only thing to do, he said.

And all I could think was: What if there is no paradise?

Jonathan pinged me one morning later that week.

Jonathan: I think you need to take a business trip out here, to set up a US office. That's as good of an excuse as any.

Me: Jonathan, I think we have to take a sabbatical. Don't get mad.

Jonathan: What! WTF. Are you serious?

Me: I just think we should probably have a relationship when we're ready to. Technically I am still married.

Jonathan: Amber, this—we're ready for. Trust me. It's no different from the open conversation that we've shared and valued all along.

A relationship is what comes as a result of this.

This is knee jerk, all or nothing, left field thinking. . . . . ;(

I'm pouting.

Me: Hehe. I'd like to see that. I don't know, something is maybe bothering me too, in a way.

Jonathan: clearly

Me: It feels a bit like your affinity for me feels dependent on my leaving my beliefs. I don't want to just jump overboard because you say it is a cult, because of what you read online.

Jonathan: nope

nope

nope

You think I'm convinced because of what I read online. I knew before I had any idea about any of that, and I shared that with you over and over. You can't accept that what you're spouting has been put into you.

And like a programmed sheep, you always retreat from the things you see in our conversations together and revert back to "anyone who questions me is attacking us."

Exactly in the way that you've been programmed to do.

Exactly the way the huge list of cult things I sent you shows that that is what they do.

Me: You don't understand how it feels to walk away from this. It feels like:

1) I am disloyal.

2) I am betraying God.

3) I am going to have to completely ditch people I love, or they will ditch me.

Jonathan: I know and I don't understand and I have compassion for you because that's all I can do.

Me: 4) I will make my grandmother cry tears and tears for the rest of her life.

5) And I will always wonder if it was the true religion and I walked away from it because the enemy Satan didn't want me

to worship the true God, and I just got sucked into the devil's master plan, of tricking people.

Jonathan: No you won't. Because you're being dramatic right now, what you're spouting is coming from that programmed side of you.

Your "always"es.

And your "nevers"es.

Me: ha

Jonathan: stop

This is the result of the fear that's been programmed to keep you sectioned off from society.

WHY Amber do you think they require what they do of you?

Me: What.

Jonathan: Because it could not survive any other way.

It couldn't survive the questioning, the inconsistencies, the inquiry that comes from truth, it couldn't survive the other information and the thousands of years of other truths shining a light on it.

It can't be the true religion—if it were, it would be able to be open to constant inquiry, honest assessment, logic and intuition, but JWs shut themselves off and retrain or eject the doubters because they have to, to survive.

Me: Hmm.

Jonathan: Looking around the Earth today, it's very easy to say that fundamentalist religions are the worst purveyors of problems in our society—because they are exclusionary and fear based and they're all CERTAIN that they are right and entitled to that right because of whatever their version of their book tells them. Fundamentalism in its very essence is separatist, fear based, exclusionary, potentially violent, and always in the name of gawwwad and they usually say it like that gaaawwwwwwaad.

Me: Only in the US of A, ha.

I walked away from this conversation and thought about the things I would say, talking to my Bible students, and I realized how ridiculous I sounded. The whole premise—my whiteness, my arrogance, my gross ulterior motive—was becoming clear to me. If I didn't have the truth, what was I doing? Indoctrinating people? It was a terrifying thought. I backtracked. Now we were back to having coffee again, my Bible students and me. I was floundering between feeling like I would die at Armageddon and feeling like a hypocrite, and both felt equally bad. My students didn't seem to mind the change.

And we didn't take a sabbatical. Jonathan asked if he could send me something. I felt nervous; whenever there was a physical reminder of him, it made me want to be in his presence. But I was excited and checked the mail every day to see if it had arrived. Somehow it didn't matter if my husband might find this package and ask me where it came from, or who I knew in California. Though we both lived here, the marriage was just something that haunted this old house.

The package arrived. I e-mailed Jonathan:

Guess whose package came today! For some reason, they didn't deliver it to my house, but when I got home just now at 5:30, the lady who is our guard was wildly gesticulating to me. She has a speech impediment, on top of speaking Chinese, so

I couldn't understand what she was so excited about. I think this customs form was the biggest event of her week. I finally decipher that I have to take this form to the post office. So, I hop on my bike in the pouring rain because I cannot wait. Then it turns out she has given me the wrong post office address, so I end up having to ride down to the other one.

When I get there, they're like, no, you need your passport to get it. The problem is, my passport is at the visa office right now, because they're changing something about my visa at work. So I literally beg them, I have my birth certificate with me, but they say no way. I was almost about to offer a bribe to get my damn package when suddenly the man had a change of heart and let me have it.

Every rule is elastic here. You can never ever give up. Anyway, when I got it, it was already open, but they had resealed it in a bag, all official-like. I really like the smell of your shirt. I like it too much. Though to be honest, there wasn't much smell until I got to the armpits. You smell good!

I sent him back a package. He had asked me for a shirt that I had worn, too, and I bought him some ties from the bootleg market. I was clearly used to buying gifts for only religious men. In addition, he looked too big and too tall in his pictures to fit anything I could get for him here. And I didn't know him well enough to know what he would like.

I knew that this was all wrong, that this was going too far, but I was highly skilled at ignoring misgivings. I had been well trained for that.

decided I needed to get away and made a plan to visit some good friends from my home city. We had lost touch years ago, after I heard they had become inactive in the religion. I wanted to get away from China, to have some space to think. I didn't want to go to meetings anymore, but when I didn't attend one, people started asking questions.

My friends now lived in Mexico, in an exile of sorts. I chose a flight that was routed through Los Angeles, with a stopover; it seemed to me a happy coincidence. I wrote Jonathan to tell him.

I don't know how you might feel about me coming there, but I want you to know that it's kind of just a nice thing for me to be able to do, the whole getting away. I don't have any expectations, I know you have your life, you're busy, and I don't expect you to change anything because I'm there. I'm not coming there because you are there, but of course it always feels, like, nice to see a friend, if you would like to.

He responded later that day.

No worries. It'll be amazing to meet you in person. I'm a little split on it now, which has nothing to do with you or my wants, entirely due to the timing being off. That said I'd hardly pass up the chance to meet you!

We suddenly seemed so formal. I think we were both nervous that we would meet and find it to be embarrassing, that the person we had spoken to for this long about so much would turn out to be someone we didn't even like.

I looked up hotels online. When I started translating my renminbi into U.S. dollars, I realized that my money wouldn't go far, or maybe just far enough to be in some miserable dive:

"Once in the room, the toilet seems to be bigger than the room?"

"Basic bed is clean, but torn blankets, no towel, no toilet roll."

"I was disturbed by many late night walkings, talkings, moanings from next door, police sirens, gunshots, planes flying on top, shoutings, people walking again, car horns, police sirens yet again and again, gunshot one more time (I think its automatic this time), people walking, police siren again. . . ."

"I checked out first thing, 7:00 a.m. in the morning, and moved to a decent hotel nearby. Thank God I am alive now, writing this review."

I decided to take one that cost a little more.

I packed my suitcase. My mother-in-law was visiting right at the same time I was going away; she was arriving the day I was to leave. I told my husband what a great thing it was that the timing worked out. With me gone, there was space for her. I tried to act friendly and normal when she arrived; I traveled to the airport to get her. I wondered if he would tell her he was now married to an apostate. She did not know who she was talking to as we sat in the back of the cab.

didn't sleep much on the plane and I rushed through customs and into the bathroom to splash some water on my face and put some foundation on. I took a long time, and Jonathan was waiting out there for me.

I walked up the ramp and saw through the windows at the top of the wall a glimpse of a palm tree, and I remembered the time my dad had taken us to Los Angeles to see Disneyland. It was the first time I had smelled air like this, seen trees like that.

I exited and saw Jonathan immediately. He was so big, he was so much taller than I could have pictured, he was so large compared to the proportions of China, and he had gained weight since the pictures he had sent. I said hello, and I felt not only shy but also surprised at this feeling I had, as if I were being pulled toward his body by some invisible force. I did not expect to feel attracted to him; I knew that the Internet distorted things and that in real life everything would be different. But it wasn't. I think that I had already made up my mind that I would love him.

He took my suitcase and loaded it into the back of his SUV,

and drove to the hotel. We got as far as the elevator and he pushed me up against the wall when the door closed, our bodies pressed together hard. We did not kiss, we just held each other. I touched his hair; it was soft and fine. On his clothing, there was the familiar smell of that T-shirt in my closet at home, pushed way to the back. Everything that had seemed curious because it was made up of pixels and formlessness and distance now felt dimensional, with a life of its own.

spent the entire twelve hours of the flight back to Shanghai awake. I never talk to people on planes, but this time I was relieved that the man beside me wouldn't shut up. First of all, because it was clear he didn't care whether I was listening. His arm creeping too far over our shared armrest, he told me about his wife from the time the plane lurched up until the first meal came, then over reheated chicken in sauce and turbulence spilling our cups of wine, he droned on about his love for her. Then when the tables were cleared and his Bloody Mary was set on the tray, he described their three beautiful children.

I half listened as he spoke, thinking about my friends in Mexico. With them, I had finally been able to talk to someone from my world about the doubts I had hidden for so long, and it had felt forbidden and pleasurable. It was empowering to know that these friends I had known and cared about so much had also lost their faith, and we wondered if there was some latent thing in the three of us that had brought us together, back then. I felt less alone, armed with the realization that life could go on without this organization to tell me how, and that the path forward, though it felt impossible, had been undertaken by others and not only by me. My friends were happy, their lives still had meaning, they were still the same people I had always loved. The week was already like a distant dream, though, fading in the face of the immediate future, the things I had to figure out.

Around the third hour, the man passed me one of his earbuds—an intimate act that on better days would have repulsed me. I gingerly graced his residual earwax with entry to my ear, and he launched into a song-by-song retrospective of Alanis Morissette's *Jagged Little Pill* album. It is the only album that runs the whole gamut of love, he told me. It's genius, he said.

"How about yourself?" he asked me when he had expounded on them all. "What song are you here?"

I lied and told him I was single, but that I had been visiting someone I loved in Los Angeles.

"Oh, well, 'Head over Feet.'" He gestured, as if it were obvious, to the earbud in my right ear.

Yes. If every love song has been written, there must be one for a situation like mine: a married missionary living in China, returning after having had sex with a man she met online, who had, over the course of a year, systematically deprogrammed her from her religious indoctrination.

The cursor on his laptop progressed downward to the next song, and he closed his eyes and mouthed the words, its tinny beat audible over the plane's thrum.

It was the first time in over ten years I had presented myself as an individual, as a person outside my marriage. It was a lie, of course, because I didn't yet know how to exist outside a ligature of two people. These arrangements were made by God, and this many years in, I didn't have the imagination left to think anything different. I couldn't even keep up the use of the singular when I told this man lies about my life in Shanghai; I kept having to amend my *we*'s to *I*'s.

"Ironic" now vibrated my eardrum. I readjusted the earbud and wondered what the apartment would smell like when our scents resolved themselves and my husband was no longer there. Or I was no longer there. Would he move out or me? Who would fix the clogged drain?

Thinking about the practical matters helped me to not think about what this meant for my life. I started to worry about the complexities of trying to make a new home in a place that wasn't my home, and the man fell into a light snore, the earbud drooping down from his left ear pathetically. What would we do with the stuff in my sister's basement? The last day before we moved to Shanghai we had sealed up our life there for a future time: the kitchen chair legs entangled, the boxes nudged up close to each other, the glassware nestled into the towels, all padlocked in to keep it safe for our return. When you commit adultery, you don't think about the things in locked rooms until later, the shared physical objects that belong with each other: let no man put apart the forks and knives, spices and rack, sheet and pillowcases.

Or, for that matter, you don't realize that the kids you are aunt to you will never see again. That you will abruptly lose touch with the mother-in-law who was more of a mother to you than your own. Thirty thousand feet up, I thought about the disposal of our life while my husband slept down on Earth, in our pink apartment in China, unknowing.

This man who wouldn't stop talking on the plane knew my marriage was over before my husband did. Even I wasn't sure I wanted it to be over; there was something to be said for the safety of habit. Though my choice of singular pronouns told me I did.

The plane hit some rough air and I grasped my armrest the way I would have grasped my husband's knee.

When we landed, I left the man with a quick goodbye, severing our intimacy with the unclick of my seat belt, and avoided his eye contact at the luggage turnstile.

Out in the airport terminal, the soft "sh" sounds of Mandarin bled into the haze of my jet lag as expectant gazes of family members peered past me to welcome someone else home. I pushed past the crowd of illegal drivers trying to talk me into their black cars and lined up for one of the metallic green city taxis.

Back on Earth.

A slim driver saw me and hopped out to open his trunk, which appeared to be jammed shut. I left him to struggle with the latch and slipped in across the smooth polyester seat cover, smudged dirty white from the grasps of passengers pointing out destinations. He got into the car, and I gave him my cross streets in Mandarin. After my last trip to Vancouver, I had hated coming home to Shanghai. And yet I had been the one so determined to move to China. With the fire of a death drive I had come and had begged my husband to come. Some instinct in me perhaps, bent on upheaval, had been doggedly looking for a way out of the life I had been living, knowing that in order to do it, I had to not see it coming. Freud had not failed me: this adultery, the apostasy against my faith, they were a death sentence to my God.

The driver nodded at me through the rearview mirror, let out a couple coughs, then pushed the accelerator down, beginning his progression through traffic. I looked down at the limp seat belt I hadn't fastened, even though in the same circumstance thirteen hours earlier in Los Angeles I would have felt terrified not to. Things deemed normal by twenty million inhabitants of a place had overruled my own sense of things and changed the way I thought. China subjected me to its ways from the uneven pavement I had once laid my cheek on after being thrown off my bicycle in a collision, the other bikers gracefully pedaling around me.

The highway expanded into a horizon, yellow gray, and the skyscrapers solidified in the distance, pulling me out of the tunnel I had been in since I had left twelve days ago, to meet this man I had known only through letters on a screen. The physical foreignness of this city—elevated highways, black bicycles, science fiction neon, and the thick gray soup that sat on skin and fastened itself to buildings for days—was a curious comfort now. These objects were now the bric-a-brac of my former life, the life of the day before yesterday, when I would still have said "we," when I still had the choice of whether or not to remain who I had been.

I had made the decision without making it. I did not know what kind of robotic force propelled me to it; not desire, not lust, nothing purposeful, it was more a passive state of action. I had to do it as much as I had wanted to do it. I needed some way of bringing about my own apocalypse, because an apocalypse was the only sort of ending I understood. In our religion, there was no other way out. There were no other possible endings.

My apocalypse hadn't looked like I thought it would: no oceans turning to blood with every piece of clothing taken off and pushed onto the ground, no skies turning darker with each penetration of my body, no giant hailstones raining down through the roof, no vultures picking clean the bones of our violating carcasses. It had been a fevered drive on a dark highway, fast, muddled bodies, a shower smelling of unfamiliar soap, an earring left behind on a black sheet. The closest thing to the Four Horsemen was a Trojan condom wrapper on the floor.

But also, it had been the joy of lying in the dusty warmth of Los Angeles, a tree's shadow stretching oblong on a wall, a stranger still unfamiliar enough to feel perfect, a smile with no resentment yet formed behind it that was all for me. The mattress croaking under my skin that felt its years of starvation as he put his arms around me from behind and I finally fell just barely asleep. Semiconscious, I had pushed off every moment until his alarm went off at 6:30 to take me to the airport, and there we lay as the shadow on the wall disintegrated. The weight of his arm wrapped around me was my doom, and it had felt wonderful. My end was not the fornication. It was the pure joy of feeling love again that was the sin there was no return from.

My driver had now pulled up at the rusted gate of our apartment complex, and he looked at me again in the rearview mirror, asking me if this was the place. I looked away so as not to see myself in the reflection and directed him into the driveway of the third block on the left. He stopped in front of the pink building and I paid the fare, eighty-five RMB, no tip. They aren't allowed in China.

I hauled my bag up the stairs, banging it on each concrete step. My husband, who had told me before I went that he did not love me anymore, always carried our bags.

I unlocked the dark green door. He wasn't home. I put my bag down and sat on the sofa. My fingers went to my earlobe, without its earring, and I waited.

found an apartment of my own. To my surprise, I liked it better than the pink apartment. My husband refused to be the one to move out. He seemed so well versed in the rules of marriage breakup, I wondered how he knew so much. I obeyed him because that was the submissive thing I had to do, this was expected of me, I was the one who should rightfully grovel and slink away somewhere, to move my twenty pounds of things in a taxi cab. Two years had passed since the last time I looked for an apartment, but the agent remembered me, the Taiwan girl, from the last time we had looked, and he asked after my husband.

The people I knew, friends in the congregation, people at home, they had already heard about what happened, that I had left my husband; they were shocked. I was a pioneer missionary. How could I do that to Jehovah's name? I was now all those things they were trying to shield me from becoming, the things they were trying to prevent for me, the things the men at the meetings and conventions warned us against becoming: a fallen woman, a Jezebel, a harlot, worldly.

I deserved this, I knew that. It was terrible what I had done. I cheated on my husband; I carried on year-long conversations with someone I had never seen. But, for some reason, if I was honest, I didn't feel as bad as I thought I should. I had done wrong. But I had also done what was right.

Some people will know what I am talking about. The husband admits that he doesn't love the wife. The wife has no more respect for him. The husband says that the wife is not womanly. He says she walks like a man. The wife tells him he is weak, and that she cannot bear it anymore. The husband and wife feel like they are half alive together, everything is closed down. The wife and the husband thought that they were moral, thought that they were good, but they were good on their own, and together they have become awful. The duty to do right has skewed everything to wrong, and there is only one thing now that can be right. The wife commits adultery, without planning to, without enjoying it, without shaving her legs or wearing nice underwear. And she discovers that this adultery, this thing that is so wrong, when it is over, when she is there confessing to it, is the one thing that she has done right, because she sees in her husband's eyes that deep down, he is thanking her for being the one to do it. Though he is angry, he admires her bravery.

And he is shocked at her strength, that she would give up paradise to be away from him.

God says that what he has yoked together, no man can put apart. It is the woman who must.

One of the last times I saw my husband, when he dropped off a handful of things I had forgotten in the pink house, I felt relief. People underestimate the power of this emotion. Though there existed inside me no small doses of shame, guilt, and self-condemnation, they were held at bay by the deep pleasure of shedding a terrible burden. It was only physics, really.

And I felt exhilarated. I was scared of who I was, of what I had in me to do. But I felt so much better now. I had done the wrong things. Yet I resolved that if ever I had a child I would tell them: when things that are right feel wrong—it means they are wrong.

Though I had managed to find a home, I had no visitors. A TV camera crew once came, to interview me for a show about foreigners who spoke Chinese and lived in Shanghai. Yes, I live alone here, I told the camera.

They filmed like a forensic crew, preserving clues in every corner of the apartment, including my closets, into which I had stuffed all my mess. Then they went out into the hallway, to get some B-roll. I didn't know what to do for the camera and felt self-conscious standing there, so I suggested that I say hello to my neighbor. The show's host rapped on the window of the older lady who lived next to me and always greeted me as I passed. The camera was poised, ready to capture her; she opened the window with a confused glare.

"*Ni hao,*" said the host. Then, in Chinese, "We're here to ask you about your foreigner friend here in the building!"

I smiled, but the woman did not glance in my direction. She drew her head back for a moment.

"She's not my friend," she replied in Chinese, and closed the window with a bang.

I read the news in English online and saw nothing but

newspaper headlines about war, about famine, about climate change, and I was worried that I was wrong, that the apocalypse *was* coming and I, apostate, was the evil, the enemy of God, the tool of the devil.

After a few weeks, my self-doubt and fear had grown so much that I decided the only remedy was to go back to the secret weekly meeting. I had to see for myself, one more time. What if every answer they had was true? There were certainly no better answers out here. Maybe I had been wrong, maybe I had been in a fever and the fever would break and I would be able to find my way back to paradise? Also, I had nowhere else to go. This world was the only one I had ever been a part of, and I didn't know who I was without it. This was what I had learned from the time I was a child: I needed to be in the organization, or I was nothing. I knew that my husband would be at the meeting, but I was used to humiliating experiences. For the sake of living forever, they were a small price to pay.

I went to the rented hotel room and sat in a row that put me out of my husband's line of sight. I felt confused about why I was here, but also about why I was not here anymore. The place pulled at me like gravity, because without it, I was drifting, directionless, empty.

The talks sounded strange to me now, far-fetched. The *Watchtower* magazine we studied read as if it had been written for a child. I began to hear with ears that paid attention not only to the good things they espoused, but also to the things that felt manipulative and wrong.

My friend Rosemary came up to me after the talks concluded, as my husband walked out the door of the hotel room, and told me she was happy to see me. I felt embarrassed, like I was in his domain, I was the fallen woman, what right did I have to be here? Anthony, the brother who had given me my instructions for preaching on my arrival in Shanghai, looked at me with disgust as I walked toward the exit.

That night I received a text from my husband. It said that I should move away. He thought that I ought to move to London, that it would be a great place for me. "A great place for me, or for you?" I asked. He ignored the question and told me he had looked into visas, and that I would most likely enjoy the pubs and find someone else to marry very soon.

I had not told my Bible students that my husband and I had split up. I was used to keeping secrets, and I now understood the preachers who railed against homosexuals while having sex with men. Preachers are not accountable, because they are only what they preach, nothing more.

But now, I was not a preacher. And my mind had begun to think for itself. I knew that some of the things I had taught them were not true, and I felt a moral obligation to tell them to think for themselves.

I overestimated the faith they had in me. When I told my former students to make sure to study other books, besides my book, before deciding on whether to convert, because I had concluded that I might have been wrong about some things, they looked at me with a face that said yes.

Jean, on the other hand, was mystified, and her eyes betrayed a pain that I had no words to assuage.

The city had broken out into a thick, dirty sweat, as it always did in August. I spent the day inside my hot house, drinking iced green tea from a square bottle and reading about the discrepancies in the translation of the first five books of the Bible. Now that the sun had bowed below the buildings, I decided it was time to go outside. I walked down the alleyway, through the smells of overripe fruit, and into a convenience store that was air-conditioned. The fluorescent lights glared and the clerk did, too, as I stood in front of the open fridge door, fingering water bottles, to cool my headache.

I heard my phone go off, which was surprising, as my phone rarely rang these days. I put the water on the counter and the clerk barked out the price. I handed over the money and walked out into the sticky street. An old couple across the way was perched on some discarded furniture. The wife was blandly cooling herself with a broken fan, a wet cloth on her head. The husband, his yellowed shirt plastered over his belly, was balancing a sweating bottle of Tsingtao on his knee. I leaned against a concrete abutment and pulled out my phone.

There was a text message from a number that wasn't in my contacts.

Hi Amber, this is Steven, from the party.

I am wondering if we could meet with you in the coming week.

When is convenient?

It was the elders.

This wasn't about leaving my marriage; I had already confessed to that in front of the panel of three elders so that my husband would be free to divorce me, and had miraculously been deemed repentant enough to not be disfellowshiped. This text meant they knew something about my doubts, too, which was much more serious. Apostasy trumps adultery in the spectrum of sins. What had they heard? I wondered. I racked my brains to think of who I might have said the wrong thing to. There was Rosemary, whom I had met with for a drink a couple of weeks before, after the last meeting I had attended.

"Just tell me what is going on, Amber," she had said in her Sydney accent. "It's okay, whatever it is."

I had spoken evasively and said that I thought it was better if we didn't talk about these topics; I knew that revealing any whiff of disagreement could get me branded an apostate. Then, to my surprise, she had said that she was pretty sure she felt the same on a lot of matters, in a way that I knew what she meant.

I started with the bare minimum: there were some things I had been researching, and it just didn't add up for me anymore, though some of it still did, of course, and it was all kind of a confusing mess. But the wine fueled our mutual apostasy—

and Rosemary agreed with me over and over again as I told her my dilemma. I felt deep love for her, across that table from me. I stared at her dyed black hair and the red lipstick she always wore. I was in awe that she had felt this way long before I had, without anyone having to argue with her to make her see. Without having to leave her husband. She was the only person around me who knew how I felt—what it was like to be warring inside between two worlds, two worlds that were a conceptual fabrication of some men long ago, two worlds that didn't exist for people on the outside but that you knew like your own body from the inside. Here we were, having to take a side in a situation that existed only because we had been born into our positions. There was the supposed wrong and the supposed right. We were in the middle, but there was no middle ground.

We finished our happy hour two-for-one wines, having arrived before 6:59 at the bar to be able to claim them, and kissed cheeks goodbye. I waited until her slim skirted figure had gone around the corner to wonder how she stayed in it, when she was just like me.

She wouldn't have told the elders. No way.

Who else had I talked to? No one, I think? My Bible students, yes, but how would the elders find out about that? Was it because I called it a "fucking cult"? Did my husband tell the elders? Possibly.

The elders and I arranged to meet on Wednesday, my day off from work, at the Starbucks on Nanjing Road in the center of the city.

The sun was bright when I woke up that morning; the usual

haze had lifted. I rode my bike to the coffee shop, feeling terrified. I arrived outside the building and locked my bike to a tree. I grabbed my bag and went upstairs and out to the terrace to look for them.

I saw the two men sitting on the same side of a table, a chair open for me across from them. They'd already bought me an iced coffee. I sat down, thanked them for the drink, then stirred with the straw, taking a sip of watery melting ice.

After some awkward small talk, Brother Steven started.

"Amber, we wanted to meet with you today because we heard about some things that were said." He cleared his throat. Brother Richard seemed to be staring just past me, as if eye contact would have been too invasive.

"We are here to encourage you, please don't feel nervous. We want to give you the help you need."

The sun was bright, like an interrogation lamp.

"Do you know the conversations we are referring to?"

"Um, I'm not sure."

It turned out to be Jean.

A few weeks ago, I had had coffee with her, to explain that everything in my life was changing, and why. When I said I couldn't study with her anymore, she had told Emma, and they had arranged for another sister to take over. Jean, not knowing that someone who did not believe in the books I had given her was the worst crime that a Witness could commit, innocently told this sister that I had told her to question the things in the books.

I explained to the elders that when I'd felt I couldn't study with Jean anymore, I'd had to give her an explanation.

"Yes, of course," said Brother Steven. "Now please tell us exactly what was said."

I thought for a moment.

"I told her to question what I had taught her. That there were some things that were not as I thought they were. To use other books, too."

I told them the truth. I had been trained to. My words were like murk in the humid air, surrounded by the light chattering voices of the worldly people. I stopped there. I knew that the more I said, the worse it would get for me. What I did not mention were the stories I was beginning to hear about how the policies of the Watchtower Society were protecting brothers accused of sexually abusing children. I also did not say that I could not morally stay in a religion that mandated people to die rather than accept a blood transfusion because of an incorrect interpretation of an ancient law. I didn't get into the fact that we were elitists who had divided the world into "us" and "them." Or that we were nothing more than salespeople, selling a myth and an illusion of love that was in reality conditional, withdrawn at the first sign of nonconformity.

I took a sip of my drink. The brothers seemed less shocked than I had imagined they would be, and didn't ask for more details. I wondered if they knew what things I was alluding to. Had others had these doubts, too? Or maybe these brothers had doubts of their own but pushed them away for fear of what the consequences would be of thinking them through to their conclusion. It was a lot, to lose your life as you know it. The price I was paying for thinking was a steep one.

In the short silence that followed as Brother Richard wrote

on a notepad, I thought of how the three of us white people at this table were criminals, breakers of the laws of the People's Republic of China. I had come to China with the understanding that there was the possibility that I might be arrested for my illegal preaching. But instead I had become a dissident. In the middle of the day, I was sipping coffee with two men who looked like any of the thousands of expats one sees around Shanghai, men with whom I was supposed to live forever in godly happiness, being sentenced to death for disagreeing with the organization. Behind their kind tones and words lay a violence. The destruction of my life.

They opened up a paper-covered Bible and read some scriptures about apostasy to me. They urged me to pray and repent, but in the meantime, my thoughts were dangerous to others, they said. I was to stay away from the congregation.

Faced with death row, most criminals would give anything to go back, to undo what they had done to warrant this unalterable punishment. Part of me wanted to tell them I was wrong, that I had been crazy, to beg for forgiveness—anything to return to the safety of certainty, to be like them again, to be able to go for hot pot with Emma after this, to keep seeing the people I loved, to have my family, to know when I woke up in the morning what it was I was supposed to do with my life, to know that I would never die.

But there, buzzing behind that panic, was the low electrical current that had been running through me for the past few months: the thought that we were all wrong. It wasn't the truth.

They were right, I was dangerous.

had no one to talk to here, now that I was shunned.

It happened with surprising speed. Word traveled fast, underground. I had been deemed "apostate." There was no return from this; it was the one sin that God would not forgive.

You have heard of the five stages of grief, perhaps. There are many stages of shunning, too. Though all of us knew what the end result of this had to be, some found it easier to drop me than others. Shunning is a messy, bitter process.

I was at work one afternoon the next week and my phone rang; I saw that it was Jay. He rarely called me. I picked up and walked back into the studio, where no one would hear me, because I assumed it would be a significant conversation. His voice was tight with anger and haughty with the unacknowledged pleasure he felt in speaking down to someone who is low.

"I am calling to let you know that you cannot speak to Emma anymore," he said. I wondered why it was him telling me, and not Emma, but I supposed this was one of those occasions when the man did the speaking for the woman. I was a little stunned but couldn't really argue with him. I knew the consequences for not believing. I was surprised at the swiftness, though, and that there was no goodbye from my friend. But these few barbed words, which he had reserved for an occasion like this, were enough to make me a little less sad to see him go. Emma had always been the kind one. Maybe that's the reason he was the one who made the call.

My husband was angry at me for upending his life. Because of me, he had been removed as an elder. He had been humiliated because he had a wife who would not listen, who would not submit. He began to tell people terrible things about me. That I was not submissive, that I was not loving, probably all true. At least the part about me calling it a fucking cult was. Somehow, I heard about his complaints. His way of getting over our life together was to obliterate me. But I already did not exist anymore, for them.

Rosemary and her husband, Mani, boldly invited me over for dinner. It was as if my apostasy had attracted them. They wanted to save me, because keeping me in would mean that they were right to stay in, too.

After we ate, Mani put on a Jack Johnson album, and as Rosemary went into the bedroom, he asked me to tell him about my doubts. I was too afraid to get into it, because the elders had said that if I talked about it with anyone again they would have no choice but to disfellowship me formally, which is a far more binding punishment than just being told to stay away. Though apostasy is considered the worst of all sins, the only one for which there is no forgiveness possible, and is normally the swiftest route to being kicked out of the organization, Shanghai was like the Wild West of our religion, and miraculously I had not been formally disfellowshipped by the elders, as I most certainly would have been at any congregation at home. The elders had given me a pass, perhaps because they were younger than many elders at home and had been my friends, and in their isolation from the organization, they might have themselves become a little less invested in its authority. But one more step over the line, I knew, would leave them no choice. It would be over for me. At least if I was not disfellowshipped, perhaps some people in my own family might still speak to me on occasion, though it was still not likely—apostates were terrifying people.

Without saying the things that we knew we both understood to be wrong about our religion, Mani asked if he could make a suggestion.

"Stay in," he said. "You can still go to the elders and repent. Being in the truth is still the best way of living, and even if it's not all true, surely it's closer to true than anything else."

He had been reduced to hedging his bets. And no wonder, since leaving was unbearable in many ways. We would lose our identities, our history, our families. And beyond that, we who had been raised in this did not recognize that we were more than what we believed. Without the belief, there was only oblivion.

This couple had a happy life; they had managed to find a way to go along with it. And now, my apostasy was like a door opened, and they were bargaining with me, because my leaving threatened the life they thought they had made their peace with.

And finally, one day, they stopped calling, because for me,

pretending was impossible. However uncomfortable leaving was, staying was worse.

I wrote to my grandmother, because I thought that I owed her the dignity of telling her that my marriage was over and that I was leaving the religion she had brought me into, without, of course, telling her entirely why. I can't remember exactly what I said to her, but I remember that I never got a letter back. Years later, when I had a baby, I visited her city and asked if she would like to meet her great-grandchild. She said yes, then canceled two hours later without explanation.

My best friend in Vancouver took me for coffee when I was on a visit home. I was surprised at this, because word had reached my old congregation that I had left the organization, and to be seen with someone thought to be an apostate could be very bad for her. But I knew my organization well enough to know that she was using the loophole of "encouraging" someone who has left to come back. I admired her bravery and respected her for it. She didn't encourage me, though, because she is smart and could see that I could not be unconvinced. She begged me to tell her what it was, why it was that I had left. I couldn't. I knew that she did not want to know, though she asked and asked. If I told her, it would confirm to her my apostasy, my mental defect, my Satanic mind, and I would never see her again; not even loopholes could survive that. I wondered, too, what was in the back of her mind. But there was a wall between us and these subjects, and without that wall, we would all be dead. As it stood, only I was.

Sometime later, my sister sent me an e-mail:

Let me beg you, Amber . . . there is nothing too big for Jehovah to forget about if you ask him. As the giver of life, he has the right to tell us what to do, as much as we may not like it, or "get it." I want to live forever with you—the way Jehovah intended . . . all of our pain healed. Did you know that JWs are selling everything in Brooklyn and getting out? They will be gone from there soon. The same thing is happening in a lot of major cities, in Britain, Brazil, etc. And with the insanity that seems to be ensuing in the U.S. . . . it seems not a long shot to say that world chaos may be right around the corner. Basically, there is a call out now in Jehovah's organization to reach out to anyone who we may know that was formerly a Witness—and this keeps being repeated—that if you are going to come back to Jehovah, NOW is the time and not to delay.

This will be last time that I reach out to you regarding this.

I wish you the best.

Everyone else I knew just vanished. It took surprisingly little time to lose a life's worth of people.

had exited without an exit plan. I was an ex-preacher, stuck in China, with no education beyond high school, no profession, no home to go back to in my home country. I took stock of things:

Things I had lost:
— family members
— all of my friends
— my future
— my past
— my life with my friends and family in it
— my faith
— my certainty
— my hope
— my purpose in life

Things I still had:
— a rented apartment
— a job, in China

— people at my work who knew I existed and would
notice if I disappeared, at least
— some clothes and bedding
— two pots
— books
— hockey bag suitcase
— bicycle
— my health
— IKEA towels
— a couple thousand renminbi in a shared bank account
— people who listened to my podcast

And a man who I think loved me, across the ocean.

I couldn't help but wonder which of these things would be gone next. Hopefully it was the IKEA towels.

was able to see how religion became a thing.

Certainty delineates things. The people of the world, the people who were bad, wicked, ungodly, Satanic, told me who I wasn't, and that, by default, had defined for me what I was— the opposite. The good.

And now that I was one of the world, I had no idea who I was. Strangely, I didn't feel that different, though everyone thought that I had changed. My continued presence each day indicated to me that I was more than this belief, but to the people I loved who were in this organization, I was only the belief, or the lack of it. I was now nonexistent to them, even to my own family, a person erased from their lives. It was bewildering. And the loneliness confused me. I had been surrounded by people at all times, in my religion. I missed my friends. If there was no witness to my life, did I exist?

I needed to see Jonathan again.

"It might not be the best time for me, but I'll see if I can clear up some time in my schedule," he told me when I asked him about dates.

He had said this the first time I came, too. There was always some trepidation, some retreat when I was about to come to be in his presence, in spite of all his longings when it hadn't been possible.

I had heard from him less lately, or maybe it just felt that way because I had so much time on my hands now. His work had gotten very busy, he said, the script he had been working on was going into production, and they were having meetings and working on revisions now, nonstop. I was already picturing life together, so I tried to busy myself with that. I was sure that he loved me, everything was so magical between us. The months of talking had exploded into love when we were in front of each other.

I began to look up flights while I waited for his response. I reasoned that if I went there in person, we could cuddle when he was between work stuff. Also, I was trying to come up with an exit plan. I no longer had any reason to be in China, really. I needed ideas for how to leave and enact a plan before I was stuck here, aimless forever in the purgatory halfway between my old life and the future.

One thing I knew I needed was money, or at least an income. I had thought the world was ending and had gotten by on part-time jobs my whole adult life, so I didn't have much in the way of savings (no retirement funds of any description for that matter either—I had thought I would never get old). My job at ChinesePod did not pay much and would certainly end when I left China. I decided to start a business, since I was going to have to support myself wherever I ended up. I figured that my way out lay in working the angles I had. I would be an importer/exporter. I would use my Chinese and look for things to bring to China or bring out of it. I had random thoughts like "Do they have cashews here?" and "Would Americans eat moon cakes?" Once, in a café in London with my husband, I saw wooden utensils—knives and forks and spoons. They seemed like a great idea, an alternative to plastic; it seemed to be just what the world needed. I was sure that they must be made in China, everything was now, and I searched and searched until I found the factory. Sam, the factory boss, wrote me back and said that I could buy them, I could become his North American distributor, but it had to be one container's worth. I asked for a box of samples and thought that Los Angeles was as good a place as any to launch my product. I could try to get some clients there, then make an order.

I began to spend my free hours searching for restaurants, distributors, grocery stores, ice cream parlors, and other places that might be interested in this compostable cutlery, which was still a relatively novel idea at the time. I bought a long-distance phone card and made cold calls to explain what I had and to see if I could send samples. Surprisingly, people were interested, and asked for samples. Sometimes people asked if I wanted to leave a message. I could not; how would they call me? I decided I needed a business card but couldn't really have one without a phone number. So I asked Jonathan if he could help me get a U.S. phone number, and he immediately went to the store and bought me a prepaid phone with a 310 number. I called my company Ecoware Biodegradables and printed five hundred business cards, along with a flyer. I enclosed them with the samples I mailed and told the business owners that I would be in Los Angeles soon, and could we set up a meeting? Hopefully they didn't call the number, because it wouldn't ring here.

I e-mailed Jonathan here and there, between all of this, to see if he had time to chat, and he often had no time, he was rushing out the door, or slammed with work. We used to talk every day, twice a day, at least, even if he was busy, but many days now I didn't hear from him when it was evening there, nor the next morning.

I started to feel insecure, like he was hiding something. That he no longer wanted me. This made me reach out more.

Sometimes he would have a moment to talk, but I started to notice that he seemed less warm. It made me reach out more, again. What had felt natural and easy before had now become weighted and filled with anxiety. Was I being too much? Should I be less available? We had been so open, we had talked about everything, so I felt like I could talk about this. I wrote him an e-mail, telling him that it felt like he was different toward me, and that I missed him.

No, he said, I am just busy.

But it doesn't make sense, I said. You always have time before bed, at least. I just want to be close again.

We are close, he said.

I racked my brains to try to understand what had changed. I talked to my workmate about it, and he said that I should just ignore him for a while, and that would make him come back. But I couldn't ignore him; he was my lifeline. He was the only person who knew me anymore. I didn't have anyone else.

Then one day he had time and was in a good mood. We were talking on the phone again, he had a few hours free.

He suggested phone sex. I didn't know exactly what phone sex was, but I was grateful for the chance at any kind of connection, even if embarrassing. I followed his lead, as I always had, as I had been taught to do with every man whom I had ever been close to, while wondering how he could not realize that an ex–Jehovah's Witness knew nothing about how to do phone sex.

"Tell me what you want me to do to you," he said.

After a pause that went on far too long, I put my bare leg up on the desk beside the laptop to try and get into the mood. I leaned back in my chair. Sex on a phone felt really abrupt.

I started out too romantic and realized quickly that someone greeting you at the airport with flowers did not fall under the category of phone sex. I switched gears. I wondered: What does he want me to say?

"Um . . . well, I am on the kitchen counter," I said, self-consciously. "And the sun is coming in. And you . . . put me up on the counter, and kiss me . . . ?" I could hear that I was narrating a kind of Chinese-censored movie version of phone sex, but I really had no idea how to salvage this; it was not even something I had heard of before. Did I need to use words like *fuck* and *cock*? I didn't have the vocabulary for this.

He encouraged me, but I couldn't really give him what I knew he was looking for, and I hung up eventually, feeling like an idiot.

There were so many things that I didn't understand. I looked so normal from the outside.

I flew to LA, and Jonathan picked me up at the airport again. He seemed preoccupied, less happy to see me than last time, not the same person whom I had last seen naked. He took me to his house. I had only seen it in the dark, and the layout seemed different from what I remembered. It was like the place had reconfigured itself. I saw that it was all glass across the back and looked down over the hills I had seen in that first photo. The valley below was bursting with muted colors and beautiful. After showing me where to put my things, Jonathan told me he had some work to do. As he went into his office, the door behind him slammed. I don't think it was on purpose, but it made me shudder.

I pulled out some papers and called to arrange the pickup of my rental car. I was here to try and get some clients for my business, purportedly. I had my pay-by-minute phone, I had my business cards printed in China with the LA phone number, I had an appointment with a big distributor. I waited until Jonathan emerged and asked for a ride to the car rental place. Something told me that I should seem like I had places to be.

Jonathan took me to get the rental car, and using the maps I'd printed out from Google, I drove my PT Cruiser to south-central LA to meet with the distributor who'd told me I could stop by. I hadn't driven in years and was so used to the fluid, rules-flexible style of Asian driving, I was honked at for drifting too near the other lanes. I felt stressed and alone and wondered why I had come, but in my new life I had no choice; I had to do these things on my own, if for nothing other than to keep my dignity. Jonathan told me to call him after my meeting; I did, and he was happy and excited that I was making headway.

I didn't really make any headway, but I had at least driven a car and navigated myself through six-lane freeways, like a person with something to do.

He worked late that night at his partners' house, but when he came home, I was waiting up for him; I had jet lag. He had some movies he wanted me to see, documentaries about Joseph Campbell. They would help me to deprogram. I was happy to be with him again, and after we watched awhile, we started kissing. Deprogramming was a turn-on, for us. We had sex, and later, as we fell asleep, he held me for a minute, and I felt that all would be okay again.

The next night he turned his back to me in the bed. His body was large, and it made a high wall. I was awake for a long time, and I saw the shadows that I had seen last time I was here, still there on the wall. They reminded me that I had been here before, even though I suddenly wondered what I was doing in this house in which the bedroom seemed to have moved to where I remembered the bathroom to be. But I didn't feel like I had anyplace anywhere anymore, so I reached for him.

We took the dog for a walk the next morning together, the dog that he'd rescued with the woman that he'd rescued. In the coffee shop he seemed impatient with me. I began to feel pissed off, but I swallowed it and tried to be cheerful.

I managed to hide my feelings of desperate confusion during the five days we were together, but the feelings were so pent up by the time I got home to Shanghai, I couldn't contain them.

The next morning I looked for an e-mail, a text, something, anything. There was nothing. I called him and told him I was totally confused. His voice stiffened, but I went on, heedless and reckless, my need for him barreling me forward. But he was immovable as ever, and the more I talked, the further away he became. The conversation was not long; he was impatient and angry, and then I had no choice but to hang up. He was done. Everything had changed. I had lost one more thing, which was now everything.

My mouth felt bitter, and my heart was hammering in my chest. I had made my way out of the office and had sat down on the open staircase at the side of the building as we spoke. I stared at some laundry hanging from the apartment next door that let out a careless flap. The steps, rectangular and hard under me, seemed to reject my flesh, my soft, nerve-worn body, which had forced itself on them.

And this cold concrete was all there was. I had no one to call, no one to ask, nowhere else to go. There was nowhere else that I had the authority to be, other than places where I paid rent or worked for my stay. The people inside my office had no idea who I was, why I looked so sad; they did not even know that I was out here, sitting on a fire escape with cockroaches.

I was a fraud. Had I become victim to one, like an old person so desperate for companionship she had willingly given over her life savings, because it was worth it for a moment's grace from the aloneness of living? Was anything real? The faith that had brought me to enlightenment had let me know that my whole life had been false. And so had love. Every soft touch I had felt would soon turn into a lingering bruise, purple turning to green and yellow.

The longer I sat, the deeper my confusion became. I had long been awed by how much care Jonathan had shown for me.

He had spent days and hours, over a year, even, patiently deprogramming me, learning about my religion so that he could show me what it was. Listening to every preprogrammed argument that I had landed on others and showing me a different answer to each of them. He had also given me confidence in myself, saw that I had abilities, that I had something that people enjoyed, that I didn't have to sequester myself from the world, that I could be part of life. We had laughed together constantly and collaborated to make things people had loved. He had made it his personal mission to show me that there was more of me than I knew. All so that I could take my self back. And I had it back. What was that, if not love?

But what kind of love flowed so generously, then was abruptly withdrawn?

I suppose it was that he loved me in the way he could, which was only from afar. And this was where it stopped. Looking back now, I can also see that the link between us, in my mind, for lack of any threads connecting me anywhere else, had forged itself in steel and was larger than life. How does one go about loving someone who feels like their savior? What I needed and what he could not give meant this was doomed from the start. Love comes in many forms, not all of them enduring.

And yet despite all of this, years later I still feel the lingering presence of Jonathan's love; it was the encompassing experience I had with him, even if it was an ocean away, even if the whole thing was weird. What force had brought him into my life I did not understand; I could not credit Satan anymore. But he had been powerful, and right, and had now handed me back to myself.

I had embarrassed myself on the telephone. I had pleaded. I left the conversation bargaining; I so badly did not want to hang up, to cut the only line I had to anyone. He was the one who finally said he had to go, ripping the conversation from my desperate grasp, leaving only this empty pink Nokia phone in my hand.

I looked at the laundry, warming in the sun, and realized that I had no idea how to live in this world and my instincts had all failed me. I was supposed to live in paradise. Nothing was as I had thought it was. And there was nowhere to go back to; I couldn't, because it was a dream, it was all a story, all of my life was made up, and I had awoken to this hard concrete.

There was only one other place to go where I could use my money to belong to a seat for a while—a bar down the street. I walked down the steps and on streets to get there, and the people, for once, avert their gaze from the foreign woman, because she is crying.

n the early mornings, I woke up with a gasp of air, when it came back to me that this was all real.

This waking up at dawn added many more hours to the day; a day became a challenge of sheer volumes of space that I had to fill. I used to spend all of this time talking to Jonathan, or filing away any experiences I had in order to tell him about them when he woke up. I began to realize what emptiness I was facing. Until China, all I had ever done was preach, or study how to preach, so that I could save lives. I was so accustomed to the urgency of that task that once I stopped doing it, nothing else seemed important. I was completely at a loss over how to live my life. I didn't even have a friend to distract me.

I joined a gym. Everyone was openly naked in the change room at seemingly all times, using the blow dryers to dry every part of their body. A few women with no underwear sat on the stools, and no one wore clothes in the sauna either. I went in the sauna to think, maintaining my privacy behind a tank top and underwear. Some older ladies were in there, washing their market vegetables in the water tap. One looked at me, paused for a moment, then told me to take off my clothes. A couple of the other ladies joined in, demanding that I remove my clothes and gesturing to a sign on the wall, telling me that I was breaking the sauna rules. I stared at the sign for a while, to decipher the Chinese characters, then, looking into their watchful eyes, I said, "I don't see a rule about no clothes."

The ringleader began to shout. I ignored her, sitting stubbornly in my illicit tank top and underwear. I was tired of being told what to do, and she rounded up the women, many of whom were rubbing each other's naked bodies down with exfoliants. They exited the sauna with a slam of the door. As she turned the light off with a flourish, the woman hissed at me, "Go back to where you come from." I sat in the dark for a while, listening to the drips from their bras and underwear hanging in front of the rules sign, which did not mention a dress code but did say: NO WASHING OF CLOTHES OR VEGETABLES IN THE SAUNA. I couldn't argue with her. What was I doing here?

After a daytime's worth of hours was spent, I found dark places and drank wine by myself in them by night. Wine made time speed up; maybe it would help me get to where I was going. But I had no destination. One time, a man brought me a bouquet of flowers and put it on my table, saying, "Such a pretty woman should never look this sad." I tried to romanticize my position: as the artists of Paris found themselves and their purpose over wine in the bars and cafés of their adopted city, I, too, would look for myself and some purpose, alone in the hole-in-the-wall bars and cafés of Shanghai. But I was here only because I had nowhere to go.

Later, at home, I sat out on the balcony and watched the high-rise across the way as the lights in the windows turned off one by one.

With so much time alone, I began doing self-help worksheets to keep myself sane. I found an English-speaking therapist, but she was a couples' therapist and not used to dealing with these matters. She said her clients were always women whose husbands had come to China for work, then run off with Chinese women. I told her one day, looking out the window of her office, that I was afraid that the world would end, that I would be killed by God at Armageddon. She laughed in spite of herself, then apologized profusely, telling me that her reaction had been very unprofessional and she was sorry. But, strangely, it helped me to have been laughed at for thinking that.

My friendships with my Bible students had not survived, now that I didn't have a quota of hours to fill and had lost the drive for meeting once a week in a crowded McDonald's. Even Jean I did not see, since she had continued her Bible studies with someone else. She didn't know what an apostate was, the dangers of people like me weren't revealed until later in the student's progress through the books, but I had been told to stay away from her, and I did. She didn't attempt to contact me.

I ordered books I found that leaked through the firewall online, emboldened against the censors, as I had nothing to be arrested for anymore. I might die at Armageddon, but I wouldn't be imprisoned in a Chinese jail.

I read books that explained how research, using X-rays and

cuneiform, had determined that the Bible had changed over the years, to the point where a reader in some cases could never really know what was originally said. This shocked me and filled me with my pet emotion—relief. This angry God that wanted us all killed might not have been fairly represented in our pages. I read the infamous book written in the 1980s by the ex–Governing Body member who left, and I saw the things that Jonathan had spent over a year trying to make me see. I saw more clearly that my religion had been founded with good intentions but was built on false premises, and it had morphed into nothing more than a legalistic, highly controlled group, as is often true of religions.

And then one day I looked up cults. I found an article that discussed the characteristics of a cult.

Jonathan had been right.

The most effective mind control is the kind that isn't rec-ognized by the victim as manipulation. They don't feel it; the victim believes that they are in control.

Cults are disorienting, and drug-like. They promote a belief system which is utopian and idealistic, and dualistic and bi-polar in nature. They see the world in terms of two opposite poles, such as good and evil, the saved and the fallen. There is a vision of an ideal "new life" or "new self," which members believe they can attain by following the teachings. The old self is viewed as inferior and flawed.

This worldview is the primary agent in cult mind con-trol. The actual controlling of mind is done by the person themselves, as they attempt to discipline their mind and reform their personality, in accordance with the tenets of their belief system.

It would be a mistake to assume that only weak-willed people join cults. On the contrary, it is often the more ambitious and strong-willed people who become the most committed cult members.

Well, that explains me.

Even after contact with the group has ceased, elements of the cult belief system are likely to linger in the mind of an ex-member for some time. In trying to rid their minds of the cult belief system, an ex-member is effectively trying to use their own thought processes to disentangle their own thought processes. For a while, an ex-member may exist in a sort of limbo between the cult world and the outside world, unsure which to believe in.

Cults frequently assert that their critics are motivated by personal resentment and negativity, or that they had hidden psychological problems before they became involved with the group. Victims are left with the near-impossible task of proving the unprovable. So long as the burden of proof remains with the critic, a cult can never lose.

And then, in another book:

Although some people do eventually just think their way out of the totalist system, it is much more likely that an alternate, escape hatch attachment relationship is the key to breaking free. If there is such a relationship available, then that allows a resolution . . . and a consequent reintegration of thought processes.

These experts were narrating my story, right down to the part about Jonathan! I was stunned. All of this had needed to happen in order for me to get out. Even though so much had been wrong in my marriage, I still felt shame at times for breaking that vow the way I had. But now I understood: the greater irony was that I had needed to. I had needed to commit this biblical sin to find my God-given freedom. I had needed to let someone in in order to get out. I would never have discovered my religion was a cult had I not become intimate with Jonathan. I would never have been close enough with someone to let them make me see.

How could I have stayed for so long? Why did everyone who was in it with me seem so normal?

I had been duped. We all had been. Probably even the leaders had been. Our religious ancestors had come up with a mythology because it felt better to live that way, and because the world could be a scary place. As the beliefs passed from our parents' parents to our parents to us, it turned into a bad game of telephone, and nothing resembled the premise it had started with. By the time any of us could have figured out we were in a cult, our whole lives were already committed to serving the community and upholding our faith. My entire life had revolved around it. Everyone I was close to was in it.

I had thought our religion was singular, chosen. But there were so many people like us, believers who were just as sure as we were. We were just one of a swarm who believed no less fervently than we did that theirs was the only truth.

And while we weren't as extreme as some—we weren't drinking Kool-Aid and killing ourselves, after all, and most of us were nice people—our group was not innocent. Many Jehovah's Witnesses had died from refusing blood in a medical emergency, after hemorrhaging during childbirth, or as part of cancer treatment—including many children. Even applying the Bible as a guide, it was clear that this ban on blood transfusions was inaccurate and should have been corrected—Jesus used a parable about rescuing a sheep on the Sabbath to teach that saving a human life supersedes any biblical law. We were mandating death, for no reason. How different was that from drinking Kool-Aid?

It should have been clear, but so many trains of thought were forbidden that it had become a monoculture. We policed ourselves to sustain our nirvana. We shared a willful blindness disguised as innocence and purity. But it was not innocent or simple. It takes a great deal of mental effort to hide from what one sees, whether that effort is subconscious or purposeful. And niceness does not qualify you from undertaking very dark things, when you believe in them.

I spent days surprised at myself. That I had not seen it, that I had enjoyed being the chosen one, that I had enjoyed feeling superior, more special than others. That once I had decided to believe, I believed, no matter what doubts came. I had performed mental contortionism to reconcile the irreconcilable so that I could feel comfortable. I had been "in the truth" because I was afraid of the truth.

What kind of person would I be, now that I didn't have any rules to follow? A few days earlier, I was stopped by a policeman for riding my bike the wrong way down a one-way street. He began to write me a ticket, and I pulled out twenty kuai, in a sudden, reflexive attempt to bribe him to make the ticket go away. Turned out the ticket was only ten kuai. He didn't take the money.

Bribery. Was this what I had become?

Was I a good person? The righteous war of black versus white, right over wrong, good against bad, had given meaning to my life. It was comfortable to know that everyone was wrong and you were right. I had known who I was by which side I was on. But there are not only two sides, there are thousands of dimensions to things. Living in uncertainty is humbling and terrifying. Uncertainty is pain.

And I didn't want to die. I thought about my own death all the time now; it seemed so near, now that eternity had been reduced to seventy or eighty years, or ninety years at best. I was an insignificant member of an insignificant species so full of idiocy, pathos, and desperation. We long to live, we long to do right, but no God helps us. Every attempt we undertake to find him ends in a failed experiment. When would I die? I looked out from my balcony, and a wrinkled man opened a window across the way, in his house built by people now dead.

It should have been clear to a reasonably intelligent person that some things just didn't add up. At some point, I supposed, as a child, the mental soup of fear and indoctrination I had been surrounded by formed my thoughts. I was offered tantalizing safety and acceptance, so long as I unquestioningly followed a very clear set of rules. For a child like me, that seemed lifesaving. And I felt I would lose my life without it.

But everyone's reasons for staying were different. What all of us had in common, though, was that we had all, for our reasons, attached ourselves to this "truth." If things in life challenged this truth, we changed truth, subjective and bendable as it is, to our purposes. We sought belief and mistook it for truth. We longed to see others believe it along with us so as to make it more true. Our collective acceptance of it became a self-fulfilling prophecy and made it the truth, for us. Just like any other community that adhered to a set of beliefs—Democrats, Republicans, Jonestown cult members, white supremacists, Scientologists, CrossFit enthusiasts, Greenpeace volunteers—we belonged, and it felt good. The truth became our identity, and the consequences for not believing were enormous. "The truth" became the only thing that mattered—not morality, not sanity.

Mao's zealots pushed capitalists out of windows and pulled up bourgeois flower beds because they believed that what they were following was true.

I, too, would have killed, if that was what Jehovah had asked of me.

And I probably would have yanked up flowers. Absurdity becomes truth when enough people agree to it, and to not do so then becomes what is irrational. And so we force our belief on others. We throw them out windows if they don't agree with our truth; we kill them at Armageddon in our minds as they shut the door in our face.

Only a mutiny by someone, or from somewhere, can bring some return to perspective. And it will not come easily. Because, perhaps, there is no more dangerous a human concept than that of "truth," and no more threatening an act than for a member of a community to stop playing along.

Revolutions do not come without violence.

If I hadn't come to China, I would never have even noticed. Somehow, in one of the most restrictive places in the world, I had found freedom.

The fall arrived, and the air was finally cool, the light had changed its angle, and it was breezy, though still too warm for even a light sweater. When I got through the day and the evening softened the light, I felt a surge of joy as I put on my shoes and walked through my courtyard, past the bicycle repairman and out under the dark canopy of trees on Xiangyang Road. I smiled at an old man putting on his tea to boil in his open kitchen door. Familiar songs were coming out of the window of a bar where middle-aged men were playing in a band for the lonely old men inside.

I saw a group of students walking back from the music conservatory go by with their cellos slung over their shoulders, and I crossed Huaihai Road to the part of the street that had tiny noodle shops. Halfway down the block, there was a little postage stamp park, and I sat down on the curb in front of it. Another lady was there, sitting next to me. I listened to the sounds and smelled the wind and watched the people. This night felt extra nice, because the sky was on the edge of darkness, and the people couldn't see me as they moved around their nightly tasks with unself-conscious humanity.

After a while I started on my way home and passed six boys in a circle drinking beer. One smiled at me as I passed, ours a camaraderie among those who were enjoying the outside night for the first time since the mosquitoes had left. I turned down the road that led to my home, past the big high-rise at the corner, and walked down the market street. The wind was especially nice at this corner; in the summer the people of the neighborhood came and lay on mats here. There was a man with his girlfriend, who was a little plump, resting between his legs, behind a pillar, and she was laughing, such a true and happy laugh I sneaked a little look at her happy face.

I thought about whether I was happy.

Had I been happier before I left my religion, or now?

I thought that I might have been happier then. "See?" I could hear my old Witness friends saying.

It was easier then.

And I was not unhappy now. Is happiness the currency of a life? That kind of happiness had been like a salve that shielded me from some of what it is to be human.

Of course, it is also human to crave happiness, and the easiest way to achieve it is through self-deception. It is also human to be lazy. We didn't like the world we were living in, so we made up a new one. The illustrators of our books gave us an image for it, and that made it even more true. We put cuddly pandas in it, took away from it all the kinds of people we didn't like, dressed everyone up in the clothing our leaders found acceptable, and put smiles on their faces. We imagined our houses built on cliffs overlooking the ocean, and our happy families and safe lives. We took every problem in the world and found a way to neutralize it, to abdicate responsibility for any of it.

If happiness is an absence of angst, then yes, I had happiness.

Another less obvious road to happiness, I had noticed, seemed to be a relative of suffering. And though I had not wanted all this suffering, all of this loss, it was surprising to me that this suffering had a by-product. The presence of pain had somehow bred me into becoming a more compassionate, just creature. Having lost all expectations as to what should happen, or how people must be, every tiny experience or thing or person was beautiful for what it was. Not immediately, but slowly, this suffering had bred thankfulness, appreciation for the things of the Earth that go unnoticed when one is blithely right. It had produced the opposite of unhappiness in me, though I had been unhappy at times. It was generative, creating in me a deeper, more thankful nature.

Gratitude was a different breed of happiness. It felt less happy in general, but was specific and resonant and compassionate in a way that felt like it mattered more. Because it was real. In fact, that was how life felt now, too: shorter, but like it mattered more.

There was no God evident to me anymore, though I didn't take that to mean there wasn't one; I took it to mean that we weren't meant to know. There were no men to tell me what to do anymore, there was no man to save me or to clean the clogged drains. There was no pat answer to all the world's problems. Things were not black and white, wrong or right, us or them. Everything was not going to be okay.

I was starting to hear myself, not because I knew any more than I ever had—in fact, I knew less than ever—but because there was no one else to listen to. I really didn't find enlightenment or answers when I looked outward to this planet of people, and since there was nowhere else to look, I looked inward. This stretch of time I had passed uninhabited by others seemed to have lodged itself into a part of me that held some seed of peace, as small and as fragile as it was.

I was nearly at my block now, and I took in all that I saw around me for what it was, not for what it would become in some dreamy future. If not for all that had happened here, I would not have left my religion. I would most certainly still be a Jehovah's Witness had I not come to this country and learned its ways. Perhaps I would have been happier.

But no matter what it took to get here, to this breezy corner, or how alone I was among these 1.3 billion people, I felt ecstatic to be free, to have this life. I didn't know who to thank anymore, so I thanked the sky, the trees, the smiles, the sounds— the things I knew to be true.

On a whim, I decided to call Aric, my old ChinesePod office mate. He no longer worked there. Though when we worked together he had seemed larger than life (or at least larger than me), I was no longer afraid of him. I had bigger things to fear now. We met at a bar, and he became the first person in China that I told the whole story to. He told me his dad was a preacher, too, back in Oklahoma.

When we left he offered me a painkiller he had bought on the black market. He knew I would need it.

I felt like a foreigner even when I was with the people who spoke my language and came from where I came from. I didn't know what people wanted, what they talked about, what they did with their time. I had been taught my whole life that worldly people would chew you up and spit you out. That they were not like Jehovah's people. That they would hurt you.

But, whatever, I was already hurt. I was already alone. What worse could anyone do to me?

Also, I had done this once before, coming here to this country I did not know. I knew how to be a foreigner. Maybe I could do it again.

The only place I was not alone was at work. I started by sitting at lunch with everyone, though I felt awkward. I sat as an observer; they didn't know they were my teachers. I listened to what they thought about politics, about the Internet, about topics I had known nothing of. I listened, mostly silent for fear of embarrassing myself, of revealing that I was not one of them. I wondered whether I was a liberal or a conservative. I wondered what I would have studied at university. I wondered what life I would have had, what job I would have done, who I would have married, what children I would have had, had I not been living in a world that was going to end.

I began to make friends with a guy named JP at work, a Filipino American Catholic from Seattle, a pleasantly unique person who seemed to enjoy a friendship with a weirdo like me. Sometimes we went for drinks after work on Fridays, to a place with bottomless peanuts. Once in a while, being inexperienced, I accidentally drank too much and rode home on my bike, wobbly.

JP had a big, bellowing voice, and we enjoyed going to lunch together. To call the waiter over, he would yell very loudly: "*Fuwuyuan!!!*" (Waiter!), as was the practice here, except that no one has ever heard it this loud—gospel singer loud. We started going to cheap Chinese massages together on Saturdays, two hours at a time. He showed me the world of KTV (the Chinese version of karaoke), and we rented rooms with his friends and sang for hours at a time. My favorite was our Whitney Houston duets. He accepted a person like me, who mid-conversation sometimes needed to ask, "Are you sure that the world isn't ending?" Thankfully, he didn't mind reassuring me that no, it wasn't. Or, at least, not in the way I thought it was going to.

And I came home alone each day to this building in the center of this city that had become my home, in which I had to figure out who I was. I passed by the man who sat at the entrance of my complex in his little booth, and my mind returned to a book I had read a few years before, about a woman who had lived in Shanghai in this same neighborhood. She was the daughter of a landowner and the wife of a diplomat in the Guomindang government, and when the Communists came to power in 1949, she and her husband decided to remain in China to help build a new China, in an act of patriotism.

Her husband was quite successful, she was from an affluent family, and they owned a beautiful French-constructed home that was full of rare Chinese antiques. But when the Cultural Revolution started, the young Red Guards broke into her house and smashed her bourgeois finery—beautiful antiques and jade—and dragged her and her daughter away. Her husband had long since died, and his service to the country under the previous government was now part of what made her a target.

She was put into prison for seven years in solitary confinement after being accused of being a spy for the British, because of her comfortable lifestyle and the fact that she worked for a multinational company. She found out when she was released that her daughter, whom she had not heard from in all the years of her incarceration, had been beaten to death by Red Guards, who were trying to get her to denounce her mother.

The official cause of death had been listed as suicide, as such deaths often were in that era.

The woman returned to her old neighborhood and was allotted a small apartment near the home she used to own, which had now been carved up into apartments for a number of families.

These things had happened in the 1960s and 1970s, in these streets and apartments I now lived in, some of them during a time when I was alive. I wondered as I looked at the inscrutable face of the superintendent, the real estate agent, the bicycle tire repairman, where they had been then, which side they had been on—the persecutor or the persecuted? Anyone of her generation would have been one or the other, yet no one talked about it. At the core of this city was this shame, a secret that everyone knew but no one acknowledged. It manifested itself in the undercurrent of tension, in the street fights, in the wear on old people's faces. This collective guilt of the perpetrators and bitterness of the victims was a wound that endured, no matter how much the backdrop of buildings rose higher and higher.

There is a way to live with this guilt, and I knew this now. Persecuting in the name of something felt different. Doing wrong for the sake of the right, like some chemical in the brain that can block pain, lets us live with it. Ideology makes us do terrible things and believe they are right. Better. I was no different.

There had been a man in my congregation in Vancouver who was gay, though I didn't know he was gay. Call me naive or just chalk it up to my not thinking that deeply about it. I hadn't realized that there were gay people in our midst, because gay people were unclean people, people in the paragraphs of our magazines, like the apostates. They were not people we knew. We were told over and over again that it was a choice, being gay, and that it was a sin not any different from adultery or stealing or drunkenness. If you indulged yourself in it, you were making yourself an enemy of God.

Dale came to the meetings sporadically; an elder in the congregation took him under his wing and tried to encourage him. Encouraging him in our world entailed picking him up for meetings and taking him out in the preaching work to make sure he didn't become irregular. There were times when Dale looked ashen and unshaven, and times when he stood the elder up.

After months of this, an elder walked to the platform during the Thursday-night meeting. "Dale Thomson has been disfellowshipped," he said into the microphone. I did not know why, and did not ask, as we were constantly counseled not to gossip. We accepted that he had been judged unrepentant for whatever sin he had committed. We did not question the elders' decisions—they were God's appointed leaders of his flock. A scripture was quoted to back up the practice of disfellowshipping, as all of our beliefs were. We were to not "even greet such a man." Dale became "such a man."

As I well knew, the only way for Dale to get back into the good graces of the community was to repent and show that repentance by attending the meetings on his own, coming in when the opening song started so that no one would be subject to his presence, as I had years before, and then leaving immediately after the closing prayer. I sat in that audience, no longer the one penitent at the back, and did not look at Dale, except to peek as I walked to the bathroom halfway through the meeting. Yes, he was disheveled. Yes, I saw him crying once, there in his chair at the back of the room. After that, I didn't see Dale for a while. If he didn't show up in the back of the Kingdom Hall, none of us would see him, since we weren't even to greet him if we saw him on the street, let alone seek him out.

One day there was news of Dale again. He had been found hanging from a noose in the forests of UBC, an area that was part of our preaching territory, the place we drove around in all day, trying to save lives. He didn't hang himself at home, because no one would have found him there, no one went to his house. Having friends in the world was as forbidden as being gay was. In no-man's-land, he ceased to exist.

There was no place for Dale in our community, and no place for him outside it. Though he had been a Jehovah's Witness his entire life, and all his friends were Witnesses, including his son, he did not have a funeral. The elders said it wasn't possible to hold a funeral for a disfellowshipped man in the Kingdom Hall.

I had felt bad when this happened, but I did nothing. How different was I than the bystanders who had stood silent as their neighbors were denounced by the Red Guard? I moved on. The community needed us to hold up the scaffolding of this world we were a part of, like our parents before us had, and our grandparents before that, and we had a responsibility to pretend that Dale hanging himself in the woods of UBC was something sad but acceptable. After the meeting, we all went for coffee and talked about Dale, then went home and numbed our feelings, to forget about him and live with ourselves.

It was like this with many things.

Who would I have been in the Cultural Revolution? I wondered. The person pushing someone out the window, or the person being pushed? And which would my Witness friends have been?

t was not helping me to keep my secrets anymore. One day after work, I confessed to my boss what had gone on and told him the whole story: that I was a fake, that I had come here as a secret preacher, that I had been underground, that I had left my husband, that I had moved out, and that all my friends and most of my family had stopped speaking to me. He was quite surprised to hear all of this. And I asked him if I could come along when he and others from the office went out together on the weekends. It was embarrassing to have to ask for a social life, but people do not think of inviting people who always have said no.

The next Friday, a bunch of us went to a nightclub. I felt as if I looked like one of the pictures in the *Watchtower* magazine, in the articles warning us not to go to nightclubs, and I felt awkward and worldly in the loud music. Other times, we went out to the soaring, expensive clubs on the Bund, or the seedy punk-band ones the police intermittently raided. At first, I didn't understand how this was fun for people. But after a while, I started to enjoy it, even for the spectacle of it all.

One late night, I heard a song I liked in a restaurant and asked my friend what it was. She burst out laughing—it was "It Was a Good Day," arguably the biggest song of the 1990s, she said.

I didn't understand most of the pop culture jokes. Someone invited me to a Kanye West concert, front-row tickets. I pretended I had heard of him. I didn't know any of the songs, and the front row was wasted on me.

I didn't know slang. I constantly asked people for explanations. They looked at me like I was from Mars.

Now that I was not a Witness, the choices for what I could do with myself were overwhelming. I could get a tattoo. I could clink my glass and say "Cheers!" I could read a horoscope, I could go inside a church, or a temple, or have my own birthday party. I could watch all the R-rated movies I had missed. I could try Lucky Charms cereal (if only I could find a box). I could curse, and I did it with abandon, enjoying the satisfaction that expanding my vocabulary with the f-word gave to my psyche.

It also occurred to me one day when I was shopping that I could now wear a miniskirt. I went into Chinese clothing shops and tried on one after another, in the end still buying the one that rose only a few inches above the knee. When I wore the skirt to work the next day, I had a conscious enjoyment of my hemline as I walked.

I was asked out on some dates, but I had no idea what the person expected of me. When did people have sex? Was there some normal practice? Was this person across from me thinking I would have sex with him? It must happen sometime, if you don't have to wait until you are married. When? After two dates? A few months? How did this all proceed? I did not know what people do. I was a quick study, but I was still behind.

One night after work, my workmate Clay invited me over to Aric's house to watch a movie. This seemed like something that I would know how to do. He and Aric were giggly when I got there, they seemed like boys, but I didn't put together why they were acting so strange, because I'd never been around someone on drugs. They later told me that they had taken Ecstasy. They asked me if I wanted some, but I was too scared to try. Aric turned on the movie, and a woman who was also there, named Emily, snuggled up to him. She seemed to know what to do. I was left with my workmate Clay, and his hands, sweaty from the Ecstasy, began to creep over my body. I enjoyed it in a way, knowing how embarrassing it would be tomorrow at work, heedless. He touched me all over, and I felt cared for again, even if it was just for this moment, and even if it was the drug.

Later, he was so wasted he could not make it home. I brought him to my house and put him on the sofa. He began to snore immediately. The next morning, it was awkward, mainly because we hadn't slept together, and I was preoccupied with wondering if someone else would have. I was the most prudish little apostate there may have ever been. I didn't feel like the devil.

I never told anyone my age, or that I had been married. I was ashamed to show them that I was not like them, that I had done things in the wrong order; so much had come before, all of which was meaningless now. I wanted to count my age in dog years, every seven equaling one, because I was so many years behind in life.

But I had my teachers.

Jenny, who gave me books about Martin Luther that she got as a student in Australia, the books that showed me that there was another way of thinking about religion, and that was by thinking about love.

Ric, with whom I spent a lot of enjoyable time reading books in coffee shops, or walking on bridges at night, at whose home I slept over many nights. He was very understanding as I explained that though I had left this religion, I still feared that having sex made me immoral; God would kill me for it. He tried to make me feel better by telling me that this had happened to him a few times in his life, that women had wanted to sleep with him but not have sex.

John B., who explained to me the difference between a conservative and a liberal, who taught me about politics, and who, walking back from lunch one day at work, stopped and told me how strange this thing about me was, this childlike eagerness to learn about the world. He couldn't understand how I could be so unjaded; it was something he had never experienced in a person before.

Kristina, my first worldly girlfriend, who moved to Shanghai from Detroit for work and called out "Dear Amber!" to me in a restaurant one night, recognizing me from my podcast, which she had listened to before she came to China. She invited me along everywhere and gave me the gift of a friendship that felt like gold, all while teaching me how to have fun.

Zhang, who was always at the gym and spent hours talking about his viewpoints with me, on the treadmill next to mine, teaching me how the Chinese looked at love, and what mattered in life to him.

And later Arthur, who found every documentary ever made about a cult and watched them with me, every single one on YouTube. I learned that cult members from the weirdest to the most extreme all sounded like me when they woke up, and they were all kept in the cult with the same tactics that had been used on me. He finally freed me of all fear when he said he would piss on the altars of those religions that stole people's futures and robbed children of their right to think. (I told him that was not necessary.)

And Jean, who met me for coffee again one day and told me in her indirect way that she'd never really believed the things I was teaching her anyway. And that our friendship meant the world to her. I felt the same.

I had felt so alone, but it was being alone that had made me see that in this foreign world I knew nothing about, where I knew no one, people showed up to help. I could have woken up from this thirty-year fantasy anywhere in the world, and there would have been good people to welcome me. I knew this now. The worldly people who took away my everlasting life were the ones who showed me how to live.

ran into my husband in a café. When you are shunned, every city is a small town. I nodded at him, awkwardly, as I left the building. Not five minutes later I received a text:

Your eyes looked like the eyes of a dead person.

He was not supposed to talk to me, but vitriol is stronger than rules. I decided to take his words as a compliment—I no longer had the shine of the indoctrinated. I would die, one day, and I now knew this. My eyes showed it.

Like me, JP, too, had begun to feel that the time had come to leave China; he was ready to move on. We hung out together all the time, holing up in his friends' luxury apartment in Pudong when they went away. Here we had access to fresh air, a giant Carrefour grocery store, and a kitchen replete with oven and large fridge, something neither of us had back in our little apartments, something we had left behind in North America with disdain but now enjoyed beyond reason.

JP would make me adobo pork and lumpia, and one afternoon as we were in the taxi to Pudong he told me about something called *The Secret*. It was a popular film and then book that had become a phenomenon of inspirational self-help. A friend of his had used this secret and had achieved all kinds of untold goals. We found a pirated DVD version of the video later at our favorite seller's stall on Fuxing Road and read the packaging. The Secret, it turned out, was the law that was governing all our lives. Plato, Leonardo, Galileo, Napoleon, Beethoven knew The Secret, it said. We, too, could know The Secret that governs all lives and effortlessly create a successful, joyful life. We decided to buy it, to investigate. We were willing to try these methods, since more concrete methods for figuring out what to do with our lives weren't really working, and because while getting to a foreign country was hard, somehow getting out was even harder.

We hung out one Friday night and watched the video. It told of people who had visualized things, pinned things on boards, and made all their dreams come true. My neural pathways, formed by life in an Apocalyptic religion, seemed primed for this kind of thing, but right when we got to the climax of the video, it stuttered and stalled, fruitlessly spinning in the player right at the most important scene, like my copies of *The Wire, 24,* and all the rest of the pirated movies I had bought. We never did find out how one's dreams could actually come true, or what the board was for, or what The Secret was. But we began to visualize what we would like our lives to look like, nonetheless, mimicking the people in the testimonials.

I asked myself: What do I want?

I couldn't stay here forever. And I couldn't go back to Vancouver, a city where everyone I knew lived and that was too small for someone who was notorious. I made a list:

— *I want to live in a big city, one I like, one that has cheese.*

My favorite place in the world was New York City; it was my favorite place before I had even been there, a place I had been to only once, and where I did not know a single person. But that situation pretty much summed up anyplace on Earth for me at this point. Okay, I would visualize my life in New York City.

— *I need a job.*

Though I liked to think I would become a successful businesswoman, my business so far consisted of a set of 462 business cards and some sample utensils. So, though I would most certainly become a spoon tycoon at some point with this Secret, realistically I would need a day job in the meantime. Podcasting? It was the only thing I'd done that people had ever said I was good at. Would people outside of this place pay people for that job? Okay, I'd try podcasting. If we could visualize anything, I suppose I could have aimed a little higher, but there you have it, I am a practical person.

— *I need a place to live.*

With what I had saved, it had to be a maximum of $800 a month for me to afford it. I had no idea that this was a pipe dream in much of New York City, but nonetheless, this was my vision, and from what I could gather, it was okay to visualize even what was unrealistic. This was the power of the universe, after all. Einstein knew it.

— It would be nice to love someone who loves me, too.
This had been hard thus far in life. If the visualization couldn't make it happen, nothing would.

— And some friends.

That was all I needed.

was running late for my flight. I called my usual taxi driver, the one who, when I got into his car the first time, years ago, had proudly handed me his card, reminding me as I left that anytime I needed to get somewhere, I could arrange it with him. He had just purchased his own taxi, and it was gleaming.

He had never been late before today. After his car finally crept up from the end of the lane to where my building sat, his body was slow to get out. He looked awful, disheveled.

I had been waiting out front, idle, for ten minutes, worrying that he wouldn't arrive, but when he picked up one of my bags and noted that it was heavy, I suddenly panicked that it was overweight, that I would have to pay extra, that I would make a scene on the airport floor, having to choose which belongings to keep and which to throw away. I had moved so many times, I should have known what I needed to bring versus what should be left behind. But I was so unmoored now, I had packed too much. I needed the crutch of objects, things to take along that would be more reliable than imperfect memory, solid matter that could tie me to my history. These bits of cloth, paper, and plastic were the only things left in my life, people included, that had been around me longer than one year.

My quilt seemed like the most likely candidate for jettisoning. I knew that I could get another one at IKEA, of course. This quilt, though, was one that someone had given my ex-husband and me for our wedding, and it was the only thing other than my wedding ring that I had of our shared objects. The wedding ring that I had promised my husband I would sell in New York City and send him half of the proceeds. The quilt didn't matter. Ric was taking over my apartment, and it was better to put it back, for him to use. I was trying to leave my life, I knew that I was late, I could throw the quilt out the window for all it would matter, but I told the driver to back up and open the trunk so I could remove it, maybe because I just wanted to see this home one last time.

I unlocked the door to the apartment and didn't have time for another sentimental goodbye. The second goodbye was no place for ceremony. I threw the quilt onto the bed and ran back down the five flights of stairs.

The driver's eyes were closed when I got back to the car. He jerked awake when I pulled the door handle.

"Okay," I told him in Chinese. "Now I am very late, and we will have to drive quickly. Do you think that we can make it there by ten o'clock?"

"Sure, sure, no problem."

I asked the driver, who used to wear clean white gloves to drive but now grasped the steering wheel like it was his lifeline, how his family was doing. I remembered that he had a child.

He began to tell me, as we snaked our way to the highway to the airport, that he had developed—well, relapsed into—a gambling habit. At first, he said, he had been winning a lot. But then he lost, and now he was gambling not for the windfall, but to get out of the debt he had gotten himself into. I could see that he had deteriorated accordingly, and last night's bad luck was like dirty clothing on his body. The car he had formerly been so proud of, and kept so spotlessly clean in streets of grit, was now scuffed and had garbage on the floor. The greasy stains matched his new unwashed, unkempt self.

"Last night, I did not even come home. I just played until the sun came up. Then I had to come, I have my business to run, I must drive, if I do not drive my child will not eat."

We turned the corner out of the French Concession and onto the ramp that would connect us to the highway. In front of us was a wall of cars three or four layers wide in a two-lane on-ramp. My chest tightened in anxiety, I looked at my phone. It was already 9:10. It normally took forty-five minutes to get to the airport at this time of day, and my flight was at 11:30. I was trying not to panic but began to mentally shove the cars out of our way.

We merged onto the highway, and it was no better.

"There must be an accident up ahead," he said.

"Oh no. Do you think we will make it in time?" I asked, unable to hide the urgency in my voice.

"Yes, yes," he said, never liking to be the bearer of bad news.

The traffic began to move as we got out of the entrance ramp area, but it was stopping and starting and it was too slow.

To add to my anxiety, I noticed that my driver had begun to nod off. I watched in the rearview mirror as his eyeballs began to roll up. He twitched alert again, shaking his head. I didn't want to make a scene, but there were large trucks on all sides, and the green taxi was feeling too vulnerable.

I said something loud, a random sentence, continuing the chatter to keep him awake. But it was hard to get beyond small talk, and after a while I couldn't carry the conversation much further. I paused for a moment to think of something else to ask him and cleared my throat loudly to try and keep his eyes from slipping closed again.

BANG!

I was jerked forward in the seat, and my driver yelled in Chinese something that I assumed was a curse. He put his hands on the steering wheel and pressed his body back against the polyester seat, wide awake now.

It was a light hit, we were barely traveling at a registerable speed, and there was no damage to the vehicle in front of us, from what I could see. But it was one of those fancy, imported SUVs, and the driver had immediately jumped out, angry. He was now almost to our car, shouting at my driver. He seemed arrogant and haughty, pleased at this opportunity to come out of this luxury car and strut his status.

In Shanghai, these matters were settled on the street, not with insurance companies and checks and letters. The negotiation was face-to-face; the aggrieved party would extract money from the offender, according to his own perception of the damage done. This was a rule of the street, and the street did not favor humble taxi drivers.

My driver was out of the car now, looking at the man's bumper, where there was no dent to be seen. He begged the man for leniency. I was leaning forward in my seat now; I felt like I was the coach in the corner of the boxing ring. The driver went back to his vehicle, spitting and telling the cabbie to wait. He sat in the front seat of his SUV and was shuffling around inside the glove box or seat. My driver got back into the car and was visibly shaken. He had no money to pay this man.

Without thinking, I leaned over the front seat and said to him in Chinese, "Drive." He looked at me in the rearview mirror, shaken. "DRIVE," I yelled, "just drive!" I didn't know how to say "Put the pedal to the metal" but I tried to, saying something like "Press your foot on that thing!" He snapped to, looked up at the SUV driver leaning into his car, looked over his shoulder, then pulled out across four lanes of backed-up traffic, weaving over to the lane on the other side of the freeway. We drove for a minute in tense silence as he looked in the rearview mirror. The SUV was nowhere in sight. He began to laugh hysterically, the laugh of someone who has not slept, who has lost nearly everything, but for this moment, one moment, has finally won. His smile was broad in the wide rearview mirror, and he put his arm out the window, raised in the air.

I didn't know if what I had just done was terribly wrong, or wonderfully right. It was neither, and it was both. I really didn't know how to use Chinese well in moments of panic or anger, the curse of the nonnative speaker, so I just said to him in Chinese, "We're free!"

I got to the airport just in time, giving the driver all the renminbi I had left. I checked the two bags, which were all I had left to show for my six years in Asia and thirty-plus years on the planet. The rest of my things were left behind in the mildewy apartment building where the bicycle repairman still sits waiting for a customer in the courtyard and the guard will write about the new tenant in his lined book. The place where I began my life but would never see again. The only place where people knew me. The gift-wrapped literature bearing news of eternal life had been replaced with earthly things like winter coats and toothbrushes.

My eye-glazing peace, unquestioning contentment, and eternal life were gone, and the time ahead of me was filled with people I didn't yet know, uncertainty about the future, and, one day, death. I handed my passport to the customs officer; it bore the same photo as when I had arrived in this country. He looked up to compare my face, the only thing that was recognizable about me anymore, and was satisfied. He conferred the exit stamp with a clunk.

Many years before I arrived in New York City, a maid left open a large window of a bedroom on Fifty-seventh Street one afternoon as she was cleaning. A toddler, the son of Eric Clapton, fell out of the window, down forty-nine stories to his death.

Each day in New York City, people die from all sorts of unpredictable causes. I read about these tragedies from time to time, over the shoulders of people holding the *New York Post* in the subway. One man was crushed by a crane that fell over in a windstorm. Another person was killed by a fire escape that came loose above his head, six stories up. Though these events may make New York City sound like a frightening place to live, a city of this size can feel like strange comfort. If a tragedy happens in a small town, there's a good chance it might happen to you. But here, you feel insulated. With all of these millions of people around you, it won't be you who shows up in a tragic headline in big black letters. And with all that is behind me in China, it feels to me as if a quota of difficulty has been filled, that somehow life will make good on me now. I had front-loaded pain, and I am filled with hope; surely my tragedy was over. But life is not so orderly, nor known for being just.

I arrive in New York City just as the effects of the financial crisis are starting to hit. I don't really understand the stock market, or how bad this will be for me and many others. I am also completely naive about how hard New York can be for a person without an education, without job experience, without even one connection. But none of it matters to me right now, I am so happy to be here, to have a life to begin again. And at first, I have time. Yes, I am in a race to catch up to where everyone else is, but on the day I arrive I have nowhere to be, I have come freely, I feel welcome here. I have saved enough money for a few months' rent, and as I walk down the streets, my insides are letting out little surges of delight. I think that by getting here I have made it here, and while I haven't come close to doing that by New York's standards, looking back at what I came from, I am a raging success.

My rented room in the East Village, let to me by a sixty-five-year-old man named Robert, is large and comfortable, all for the price of $800, just as I had "Secreted." One of my podcast listeners had found it for me, through her brother, who lived across the street. Nearly every time I tell someone where I live—at the corner of First Street and First Avenue—they exclaim, "The nexus of the universe!" I don't know what they mean until months later, when someone tells me it's a line from a *Seinfeld* episode, a show I have never seen. Robert kindly provides a mattress for me on the floor, a bookshelf for my things, and a steel bar hung from the high loft ceiling for my clothes. I regret not bringing my quilt, but there is an old Cornell blanket that smells vaguely of weed.

I wake up each morning, put my wooden spoon and fork samples into little kits that hold my business card and a promo sheet, and head out to traverse the island, street by street. I am sure that America will be good to me; my bar is not high. I just want a home.

I get to know this city in unusual ways. Long before I have friends, I have deli owners. I shake hands with thousands of bodega keepers. I wait in line and chat with tourists at the disproportionate number of cupcake shops. Though I don't yet know anyone, I nod to the street vendors and mix with the people who go in and out of buildings, wondering if I will ever find one that I can enter without some pretense. Everything seems magical to me, because though they are the same streets that existed before I was part of them, when you are of something, rather than outside of it, everything feels important and interesting in a way it hasn't before.

I start midway through the western edge of Central Park and walk all day, east to west, in and out, down one block and back east again. Though people are nice, they are often very rushed and grab the sample packet as a way to stop me from talking anymore, from holding up their line. The cupcake shop owners are more generous with their time, perhaps because I look like the demographic of a woman who would buy a cupcake. I don't like cupcakes, but I do sometimes take home a deli sandwich and eat it in my room for dinner. They are so cheap, after all, and it has been so long since I have been in a place with so much bread and cheese.

My import-export business is not as booming as I had hoped it would be, and I am making no money from it yet. So I also scour Craigslist, LinkedIn, and every job board I can find, entering the meager keywords that describe what I am professionally qualified to do: podcast, Mandarin, Chinese culture expert. Not much comes back. There are very few podcasts in 2008 and even fewer jobs involving podcasts, very few jobs of any kind, for that matter, given the crisis. I apply to the public radio channel but never hear back. I pitch podcast ideas to places like the Guggenheim. No one responds. I spend each day filling out application after application, and there is nothing.

It is difficult to find someone willing to hire me. And no wonder, because though I apply for hundreds of jobs online, I haven't been to college much less have a degree, my work experience makes no coherent sense, and the algorithms spit me out before I even get close to anyone's eyeballs. But I never think I should leave or go home to Vancouver or somewhere else, because I have no other home anymore besides this one. And I can't bear to start over yet again.

Once in a while one of my old ChinesePod listeners comes to the city and contacts me through my old e-mail account, to ask if they can take me out for dinner. I say yes to all of them, and laugh to myself about the obscurity I have again now, sitting across from someone who acts nervous, as if I am a star.

I try very hard to make friends. There are a lot of things happening at all times, and anywhere anyone invites me, I go. I meet a lot of nice people. A family lets me come along to their

Christmas, the first I've ever celebrated. They treat me like someone who belongs here, and their home feels like one you would see in a Christmas movie.

I also meet some not-so-great people, though fewer than one might expect.

I go to rooftops. I go to art galleries. I go to museums, I read in parks. I sit in the majestic churches of Fifth Avenue, just to see how it feels. I go anywhere free. New York is a good place to be jobless, if you can stand it.

This is how it is, for a long time. I yearn for belonging, friends, some sense of continuity. I dream of having people with whom I have memories and who, when they make plans, think of calling me. People don't. They haven't known me long enough to think of me. It takes effort to find people when you have no people. And so I go from one random invitation to the next. I make it my job to talk to people, I work at it like an avocation, like a skill I need for survival. Many times my body takes me there when I do not want to go. But the human body knows what it needs to survive. The people in this city who have no one, who never leave their apartments, they die, one day, and someone finds them only because of the smell.

And yet I love it here. I feel like it is where I belong, even though I am miserable sometimes, even if no one notices me here. I have so much time on my hands, I walk everywhere, bike the city, it becomes my friend. Though I have no one over that bridge to go see, a distant side of any bridge is an invitation always open to me. I ride across the Williamsburg Bridge and watch skateboarders who seem too old to skateboard. I ride alongside the deafening trains over the Manhattan Bridge to read on a round mound of grass nestled under it. I traverse the Pulaski Bridge to see the sewage treatment plant, for god's sake. The city and I become intimate in this way.

I become accustomed to my life of getting by, but fear rises as my savings dwindle. Something most people don't know about New York City is that, oddly, it can be lived in for little money, if one's rent is cheap, and I am very lucky to have cheap rent. I have my routines. Breakfast, an egg sandwich for $2.50 at the kiosk in the First Avenue Park next door. Lunch, a bean burrito made in my roommate's kitchen. Dinner, from the Whole Foods cafeteria, where I choose the foods that weigh the least and so can have a leafy greens–filled dinner for under $7. Probably the most money I spend is on cheap wine, which I drink while sitting on my fire escape. There is a nosy neighbor who sees me out there, across from her apartment, and I worry she will tell Robert I am out there and he will tell me to stay inside. But she doesn't.

When I sit on the fire escape, I am grateful to have a home. But my feelings of being unmoored make me understand how fast someone can become homeless or sit screaming obscenities to themselves in subway cars. Who would come find me, if I was sitting on a street with a cardboard sign that read something about my situation? When I run out of money or places to occupy myself, will I give up and just scream at the universe from the subway? I can understand how my father took to drinking. I do everything in my power not to succumb to what I know lies lurking in my genes. To drink less, I take up smoking on my fire escape. Like swearing, smoking was forbidden in my old life, and somehow each cigarette feels like a statement.

As it happens, Robert loses his job and is now unemployed, too. An unlikely friendship, ours, but as winter comes, and I feel too cold to go outside, he invites me to sit on his office chair and watch old classic movies, or Hitler documentaries, with him. He makes a bowl of popcorn and kindly gives me half. We are two souls who share a kitchen and snacks and loneliness.

And then one day, I get a job. It is a terrible job, for a terrible company, writing online content and podcast scripts that are terribly boring. But it is something. Two years into that job, and after hundreds more job applications, I finally get another job, when a LinkedIn glitch means that the recruiter can't open my résumé, and she doesn't realize I don't have a degree until I am already there interviewing.

And finally, a helping hand here, kind people there, and nothing but sheer force of will—because what other choice do I have if I don't want to be homeless or screaming—and now it has been five years since I left China, six since I left my religion, and I feel that things are okay again, like I have a place in the world, friends, a home. I am enrolled in college at night school, I am getting my degree. My thoughts feel slow at first, after so much disuse, but they soon sharpen. I am often the oldest student in the class and make friends with the professors more often than with my classmates, as they are more my peers. I have a birthday party, my first, and have friends to invite.

In time I meet someone, I have a relationship, and we move in together. I ask him if we can have a child; I know that if I will ever have a child, it must be soon, though he does not feel ready. I become pregnant, and when the baby is born, he holds his son at the window in the hospital and says to me, "Thank you for making me have a child." And I am in heaven. Our boy's name is Karl.

I had no idea that life could hand me something this wonderful. I am fascinated by this little being, and the world becomes even more beautiful to me for the next 117 days, all of them spent with him. We are together each day and all through the nights. My life feels happy again, and when I am in the wakeful dark with my newborn I notice that I am content. Now I am part of this world, I am a person in relation to someone else, I am needed, my existence is important to this being, everything is back on track, there is love all around me, sleeping near my heart.

And then, in a moment, it is gone. The child is torn from me with a violence like shattering glass. In the handful of seconds it takes to breathe in and breathe out, he is no longer here. All that remains is aftermath. My child, a dead child, big black letters in the *New York Post,* followed by tiny letters in paragraphs that spell out a story that twists off the page and down onto the subway floor and into hell itself.

Seven years after undoing the belief that my life would stretch forward longer than human existence had been on this planet, of trying to unravel my twisted sense of time and unfurl it into something linear and finite—death has come. This making of my peace with life, of finding myself at last in some familiar place, a place that felt like home again, near to where my contemporaries were, and in a moment, it all is gone. Any meaning I have eked out of this life, any peace with my spirituality, disappears the instant I see his blue lips.

It was a hot July Monday, a heat wave, and I dropped him off for his first morning at day care, a few blocks away from where I worked. He was almost four months old. I didn't want to leave him yet, he was too small, I was not ready, but it had taken me so long to get to the point where I had stability, I was afraid to quit my job. He was put down for a morning nap at 10:30 by the day care owner and not checked on. Someone saw him kicking, but they did not go to him. And when I arrived at lunch to nurse him, he was dead. No one could tell me why, or what had happened.

My past was inescapable. It was like something that I dragged along behind me, that I kicked and flicked to get off me. But it could not leave me alone. When I thought that I was finally okay, that I had finally conquered everything my past had taken from me, I had this child who would grow up free, I had family again, I had flesh and blood to touch and talk to and hold, and now everything that meant anything was gone. Hundreds of parents had taken their children to this day care over fourteen years. But I walk in the door of the day care, and my child, left just two and a half hours earlier, the most precious gift I thanked the universe for each day, the being who had made up for all the suffering that had come before, whose life I cannot wait to witness, is limp on a change table, a woman performing CPR, his lips blue. My past was determined to take away from me what others had, with cruelty and violence. You cannot outrun what has come before.

I begin to live life in reverse.

Had I: Quit my job. Started work one week later. Been sick that morning and stayed home. Come back to the day care fifteen minutes earlier. Not had sex the night I did and become pregnant with him. Not had the miscarriage two months before conceiving him. Not stayed with his father when we had fought bitterly and terribly. Flown to Singapore to see Ric when he had asked me to. Moved to another city. Stayed in China. Suddenly in rewind, everything was certain. If I hadn't closed the door of my apartment that morning in Shanghai, I would not have a dead child.

In this reverse hopscotch, I always end up back here. My life is divided into before and after. I cannot look at an old photograph of myself without thinking: this is a person who did not know that her child would die.

This tragedy becomes my new religion, another attempt at arguing with bleak reality. I am desperate for a savior that can make me no longer the mother of a child whose heart has been pummeled by a stranger on a change table stained by all the children who had lain on it, alive. Or a Buddha that can reverse time and let me go back and walk past the day care and onward home again, my baby still in my arms. An Allah that can take the sight of my dead child from the place it replays on the walls of my eyes, every day, while the rest of the world forgets that he had ever existed. Some transfiguration to free my mind of the thoughts I have as I sit in rooms with strangers, wondering:

Have you seen a dead baby? Why do I have a dead child, and you don't? A living, chubby, breathy wonder transformed into a cold, dead, stiffening body, a trickle of liquid finally pouring out of his mouth before the nurses kindly tell you it might be time to let him go, your breasts painful and engorged with the milk he is not drinking?

I begin to understand why people concocted ideas about life and death. I now know what dread we were all trying to avoid, with our cults and religions. Even those with no religion—we were all hiding, indoctrinated, embedded with ideas about how we must be and must live so as to impose order on the disorder. People sometimes wake up one day and realize that the life they live or the belief system they carry around doesn't work anymore, for any variety of reasons. But many of us don't, because our culture (or to say it another way, cult) too fully consumes our life and extends across our world, our peer group, our country, our political affiliation, and all of our experience. We don't even apprehend this, because we are never far enough outside of it to understand what is happening.

This leaves only the upheavals, the blindsides, the tragedies, to discompose us enough to investigate just how much the environment in which we find ourselves has created the way we see the world. It is a struggle to see the truth through our indoctrination, to verify the stories told to us by the culture we have been born into, or have chosen.

And now, religion-less, childless, once again with a lost identity, that of motherhood, nothing makes sense and everything makes sense.

Reincarnation now seems to me a perfectly valid concept

the human imagination would create as a means to assuage the torture of not being able to go back and relive a day, to undo what has happened. I want to try out a different path, a different cult/culture, and see if it will lead to less anguish, because certainly no other path could have led to worse than this. I want to come back as a woman with good parents, who goes to college, who is allowed to love whomever she loves, has children who live, work she enjoys, and a home with family and friends who laugh about the old days. But most of all, I want to come back as a mother who did not leave her son to die alone, without her. I want to come back to a world that has my son in it.

I now know why people say that everyone has a cross to bear, because I feel this cross crushing me at all times, with the what-ifs and the guilt and the horror of making this incomprehensible mistake. I can understand why people want laws and rules and rights and wrongs now, because if this can happen to my healthy, happy, perfect child, chaos lurks everywhere.

Heaven as a solution is the stab in the dark that most people refer me to, and when I indulge in the thought of my boy somewhere cotton-like, white and near the sun, a place where one day I would go to and scoop him up in my arms and hug him with every synapse in my brain and nerve ending in my body, it is the most comforting of them all. And, therefore, feels the most deceitful.

What I did not know about the cost of being raised on myths is that it also makes it impossible to deceive oneself anymore. There is no way to find comfort in death. When I experienced my father's death, I had known it as something temporary. I now know only nothingness. Death is the bleak, the desolate, the scorched, the evaporated, the empty.

And I know now that I had been wrong, thinking that things are not black and white, when I left my religion. There *is* black, and there *is* white. My son was the right, his death was the wrong. The only equal to the deep, sublime love I had for this child is the dark, destructive grinding of this pain.

I had been in heaven, and now I am in hell.

I can no longer deny these poles. They are everywhere around me, life and death, the sky and the underground, the East and the West, the full and the empty, love and hate. My son's death is a battle I could spend decades fighting, my grief has the energy for a lifetime of war. But war will only lead to more desolation and ruin.

I am a person who survives things. People tell me my son would not want me to suffer in this way. I want to escape this, perhaps because the pain is too great and the culture I knew— the one of heaven, paradise, Armageddon—is one of escapism. We were saved by escape, but nothing about this is escapable. And so my mind, desperate to find a way through this, as there is no way around it, wanders to the other culture I know best, that of the East, with its ways that had been so different from my own. I look up its principles of yin and yang, and read with recognition about the cold, dark, passive power of yin—earth, rain, soft, evil, black, small. But also with lingering remembrances of the light, of the good, of the largess of yang— heaven, sunshine, hard, good, light. There can be no yin without yang, it is said, and there will be no harmony without both. I read on:

A property of the light is its brightness, which illuminates
the dark.

The dark that is night is followed by the light of day.

In each of the opposing forces, there is a small part of the
other.

In every mother there is her child. In every child, there is
his mother.

Here I see, finally, a truth that feels truer than those that
came before. The only way to find peace is to bring the halves
together to make a whole. The only way to stop this war is to
live with my son's life, and his death.

The only way to endure this loss is to hold on to the love.

In the yin, there is the yang. In the yang, the yin. On the day
after death, there was still life, though it felt to me that there
could not be. I wake up morning after morning, though I died
with my son that day. My life continues—hour after hour, day
after day, month after month—my life that against all odds
still exists, and I must live, though it's unbearable that my son
does not. And, in the midst of all the loss, I am overwhelmed
with love. The goodness I had been taught was the possession
of only those in my former religion was actually the good that
was in human beings. People I knew, people I knew only a little, and strangers all showed up out of nowhere to bring kindness, to help, to give, to hold me because my arms that were
full are now empty.

I thought that I had known suffering before, but now, I
know that suffering is not the pain one has for oneself. True
suffering is suffering for what a human being you love has lost,

for what they will never have. This suffering has no words for my page, it cannot be expressed because there is no language that can understand it. This suffering is noise too loud to hear—silent letters are not enough to render it.

Loss is loud, and love is quiet.

For every memory of my son's death, I have thousands of his life. I am in the blackest, densest, most impenetrable night, and even here, there are glimpses of light, contradicting the dark, like stars in the night sky. They are the glimpses of love.

When the clamor of grief overwhelms me, this roar that no one else can hear, I pull my way out, back to life, to my son's laugh, his smell, his fleshy cheek, his numinous gaze. This is all I can do. I carry him around in the days, and hold him tight in the nights. I walk the streets we walked, retracing all that his curious eyes saw. He is gone, yet he is here.

Knowing death makes one grateful for life. I am both desolate with my privation and full of gratitude for all that I have lived. In the absence of my son came the presence of love from all around me. And then his little sister, with a smile and fingers just like his. Though I will never know who my first child would have been, I know his love. If there is a God, this is what he gave us.

Asked about death once, Confucius answered, simply: "We haven't yet finished studying life to delve into the question of death."

The question of my son—the mystery of his death, his whereabouts—remains without answer.

And so I ask the questions of life: What force grew this little child? How did that spine and those limbs form themselves from nothing inside of me? Why did I have the power to make him, but not to bring him back? Why are the things he saw on this planet so beautiful? Why did his eyes look at me the way they did? Where did love like this come from? How, in the face of so much pain, was there also beauty?

This alchemy of life, this magical planet, they bewilder me, they awe me. But no understanding comes, any more than it did to any other human who walked this hard land, feeling entitled to explanations where there are none. I have called a truce with the unknown, and I am learning to live with the disquiet. I do not attempt to pray to a God who will not answer.

ACKNOWLEDGMENTS

Thank you to my excellent editor, Wendy Wolf, and her most intelligent and capable assistant, Terezia Cicel, for making my book so much better, for seeing the things I couldn't see, and for making it possible for my story to be in the world in the first place. Warmest thanks to my agent, Flip Brophy, for believing in me and being so good at what she does. I am forever grateful, too, to my publicist, Maya Baran, who went above and beyond in all ways for this book, and to the many others at Viking who played important roles behind the scenes to make this book a reality.

When I left the Jehovah's Witnesses, I was without a friend in the world. And now, not only do I have friends, I have friends who are like family. These friends conversed endlessly with me about this book, answered every e-mail, reviewed every version sent to them, gave feedback and cheered me on, weighed in on book titles and book covers, helped with publicity, and most of all, reminded me to believe in myself and believe I could write my story. Among these are Katherine Zoepf, Karen Emmerich, Jen Carlson, Aaron Kaufman, John Kuhner, Nic Kazamia, Lisa Brennan-Jobs, Leanne Shapton, and so many more who helped along the way in ways large and small.

These are some of the same friends-family who also helped me survive the loss of my son, Karl. It is these people that make it possible for me to hold on to some fragment of belief that there may be a loving higher power out there somewhere because of all the goodness they have shown.

The highest praise and thanks also go to Lee Towndrow, who was the very first champion of my story, frequent reviewer, coach, story consultant, and talker-down-off-ledge. Also Radha Ramkissoon, whose ever-loving ways made it possible for me to entrust my child to someone again, and without whom I would never have had the time to write this book. And of course, I will be thanking my daughter, Sevi, forever, for just existing. I am grateful for her beyond words.

Thank you, too, to Sheila Heti and Heidi Julavits for going out on a limb to publish me for the first time in *The Believer* magazine. I would never have understood how important it was to have stories like mine in the world until I received the avalanche of responses that came in from that first essay I wrote. There are so many who have been through things similar, and also so many strong, resilient survivors. I am in good company.

Finally, I want to thank my brother, Darrell Scorah, and my cousin, Nicky Whitehouse, for being the family that stuck by me—you are both gems. I'm also truly grateful to my very first friends in the real world, who only make small appearances in the book but who had a gigantic impact on my life. To my Shanghai family: Helen Cao, JP Villanueva, Dottie Fromal, Kristina Adamski, Ric Stockfis, my coworkers at Chinese-Pod, and the listeners to my podcast. You embraced me without judgment when I had no one and nothing, and helped put me on my feet again, even if you didn't know you were doing it. Same for my New York City friends-family—you have become like sisters and brother and mothers and fathers, and I'm so honored to have you in my life.

Last but not least, I want to thank Jonathan Watters for helping me see the light.

To any of my old Witness friends and family, if you've dared read this far: know that I will be here waiting for you, if you ever begin to question things. My door is open, I still love you, and I promise that a happy and fulfilling life is possible out here.

REFERENCES

The history of Christianity in China comes from Daniel H. Bays, *A New History of Christianity in China* (Hoboken, N.J.: John Wiley & Sons, 2011), 7–15, 18–21.

The quote on pages 34 and 35 comes from Mark C. Elliott, *The Manchu Way: The Eight Banners and Ethnic Identity in Late Imperial China* (Stanford, Cal.: Stanford University Press, 2001), 241.

Transcript of "Dear Amber" podcast episodes printed with permission from ChinesePod.com.

The article on pages 228 and 229 comes from Patrick Mark Dunlop, "Mind Control in Twenty Minutes," http://www.ex-cult.org/fwbo/MC20mins.htm.

The passage quoted on pages 229 and 230 comes from Alexandra Stein, *Terror, Love & Brainwashing: Attachment in Cults and Totalitarian Systems* (New York: Routledge, 2016).

The quote on page 274 comes from https://feng-shui.lovetoknow.com/Ying_Yang_Meaning.